Corruption: A Very Short Introduction

VERY SHORT INTRODUCTIONS are for anyone wanting a stimulating and accessible way into a new subject. They are written by experts, and have been translated into more than 40 different languages.

The series began in 1995, and now covers a wide variety of topics in every discipline. The VSI library now contains over 350 volumes—a Very Short Introduction to everything from Psychology and Philosophy of Science to American History and Relativity—and continues to grow in every subject area.

Very Short Introductions available now:

Available soon:

For more information visit our website

www.oup.com/vsi/

Leslie Holmes

CORRUPTION

A Very Short Introduction

OXFORD
UNIVERSITY PRESS

OXFORD

UNIVERSITY PRESS

Great Clarendon Street, Oxford, OX2 6DP,
United Kingdom

Oxford University Press is a department of the University of Oxford.
It furthers the University's objective of excellence in research, scholarship,
and education by publishing worldwide. Oxford is a registered trade mark of
Oxford University Press in the UK and in certain other countries

Published in the United States of America by Oxford University Press
198 Madison Avenue, New York, NY 10016, United States of America

British Library Cataloguing in Publication Data
Data available

Library of Congress Control Number: 2014953671

ISBN 978-0-19-968969-9

Printed and bound by
CPI Group (UK) Ltd, Croydon, CR0 4YY

Contents

Preface

Open almost any newspaper on almost any day of the week in almost any country nowadays and you will find a report of one or more corruption scandals. According to surveys of more than 24,000 people conducted on behalf of the BBC in late 2010 and late 2011 across twenty-six (in 2010) and twenty-three (in 2011) countries, corruption was the topic most frequently discussed by the public globally, ahead of extreme poverty, unemployment, the rising cost of food and energy, climate change, and terrorism. Since these polls were run at a time when most countries were still suffering the effects of the 2008 GFC (Global Financial Crisis), such results testify to the significance of corruption in the contemporary world. Indeed, a more recent (2013) survey of almost 70,000 people in sixty-nine countries, conducted by WIN/Gallup International, provides further evidence to support this contention; it identified corruption as the world's no. 1 problem.

Whether in the developing world, transition countries, or the developed world, more and more citizens are becoming aware of the serious negative effects of corruption, and are demanding that their authorities do something about it. Governments that do not heed such demands do so at their own peril. For instance, public resentment at the high levels of perceived corruption was a major factor in the overthrow of the Yanukovych regime in Ukraine in early 2014, and in the mass unrest that resulted in so many deaths and led to the toppling of the government in Thailand in 2013-14. Innumerable further examples could be cited.

Yet it is only relatively recently—since the mid-1990s—that the international community has become fully aware of the corrosive and potentially devastating effects of corruption. It is the importance of the issue that has led me to write this short introduction.

The study of corruption cannot be neatly pigeon-holed in terms of a particular academic discipline, and this brief analysis draws on the work of anthropologists, criminologists, economists, historians, lawyers, political scientists, and sociologists. But the topic is now so widely discussed and affects so many people that it would be a serious mistake to consider the work only of academics; the important contributions of practitioners in International Organizations, non-governmental organizations, and elsewhere are also considered here.

Since I have been researching and teaching corruption for some three decades, it would be impossible to thank individually all those who have helped me to deepen my understanding of this complex phenomenon. But I do want to single out the hundreds of postgraduate students I have taught in Melbourne, Warsaw, and Bologna who, over many years, have asked me challenging questions and shared their own experiences and knowledge of corruption with me. I am also grateful to the four anonymous reviewers of this project; were it not for them, there would be even more errors and oversights than there still are in this book, and for which, of course, I am solely responsible. I thank the Australian Research Council for the considerable funding they have awarded me over almost three decades to investigate various aspects of corruption, and Andrea Keegan, Emma Ma, and Jenny Nugee at Oxford University Press for all the help they have given me in bringing this project to fruition. Finally, I want to thank my wife, Rebecca, for her continuing love and support; her tolerance and understanding when I spend far longer in my study, and travel overseas far more often than I should, are deeply appreciated.

L. H.
August 2014

Preface

List of illustrations

List of tables

List of acronyms

Only acronyms used more than once or not defined in the text are included here.

ACA	Anti-Corruption Agency
AML	Anti-Money Laundering
AWB	(formerly Australian Wheat Board)
B2B	business to business
BAE	(the name from 1999 of merged British Aerospace and Marconi Electronic Systems)
BBC	British Broadcasting Corporation
BEEPS	Business Environment and Enterprise Performance Survey
BPI	Bribe Payers' Index
CDU	Christian Democratic Union
CEE	Central and Eastern Europe
CoE	Council of Europe
CPI	Corruption Perceptions Index
CPIB	Corrupt Practices Investigation Bureau
EDI	Economist Democracy Index
EU	European Union

FATF	Financial Action Task Force
FBI	Federal Bureau of Investigation
FCPA	Foreign Corrupt Practices Act
FIFA	Fédération Internationale de Football Association (International Federation of Association Football)
FSI	Failed (or Fragile) States Index; Financial Secrecy Index
GCB	Global Corruption Barometer
GCI	Global Competitiveness Index
GCR	Global Competitiveness Report
GDP	Gross Domestic Product
GRECO	Group of States against Corruption
ICAC	Independent Commission Against Corruption
ICJ	International Court of Justice
ICVS	International Crime Victim Survey
IFI	International Financial Institution
IGEC	Interpol Group of Experts on Corruption
IMF	International Monetary Fund
INGO	International non-governmental organization
Interpol	(common acronym for what is officially ICPO—International Criminal Police Organization)
IO	International Organization
NGO	Non-governmental organization
NSW	New South Wales
OECD	Organization for Economic Cooperation and Development
PETS	Public Expenditure Tracking Survey
PRECOP	Protection of the Entrepreneurs Rights in the Russian Federation from Corrupt Practices
QSDS	Quantitative Service Delivery Survey

RLI	Rule of Law Index
RUCOLA	Russian Federation—Development of Legislative and Other Measures for the Prevention of Corruption
SNAC	Southern Neighbourhood Against Corruption
TI	Transparency International
TNC	Transnational Corporation
UK	United Kingdom
UN	United Nations
UNCAC	United Nations Convention Against Corruption
UNODC	United Nations Office on Drugs and Crime
US(A)	United States (of America)
USSR	Union of Soviet Socialist Republics
WTO	World Trade Organization

Chapter 1
What is corruption?

Corruption has existed and been a problem since the beginning of human history. Corruption and general moral decay have been seen as major factors explaining the decline of the Roman Empire, while the Protestant Reformation arose to no small extent as a response to what were perceived to be various forms of corruption, including the improper sale of indulgences, in the Catholic Church.

In its traditional sense, corruption refers to moral impurity; the word itself derives from the Latin for 'to spoil, pollute, abuse, or destroy', depending on the context. But the concept of corruption has changed over the centuries and varies somewhat across cultures. It has been used in broad terms to describe any deviation from the norm that is considered improper; in the past, and to this day in countries such as Iran, this was often related to religious norms. Such usage is rare in contemporary English, and the term nowadays refers primarily to improper behaviour linked to one's official position; this is the focus of this short book. But what constitutes improper behaviour, or even an official position, is contested; the debates on what corruption means today form a key component of this chapter.

Current debates on defining corruption

A significant problem in attempts to combat corruption is that analysts cannot fully agree on what it is. At one end of the spectrum is the broad interpretation that corruption, like beauty, lies in the eyes of the beholder. At the other end is the legalistic approach, according to which an act or omission is corrupt only if explicitly identified as such in legislation.

The definitional confusion can be demonstrated using two significant examples. First, there is no definition of corruption in what the United Nations itself describes as 'the only legally binding universal anti-corruption instrument', the United Nations Convention Against Corruption (UNCAC). This is largely because those who produced UNCAC could not agree on a definition. Second, the world's leading anti-corruption INGO (international non-governmental organization), Transparency International (TI), has for most of this century used *two* definitions—but now fudges the issue. For its best-known product, the annual Corruption Perceptions Index (CPI), it used until 2012 what is still the most commonly cited definition, 'the abuse of public office for private gain'. This definition is similar or even identical to that used by many other agencies, such as the World Bank. But in all other contexts, TI defines corruption as 'the abuse of entrusted power for private gain'. The principal difference between these two is that the first requires an officer of the state to be involved, whereas the second, also favoured by Interpol, is broader, and allows for the miscreant behaviour of, for instance, senior executives of private corporations and even corruption purely within the private sector (B2B, or business-to-business—see Figure 1). In 2012, TI stopped defining corruption for its CPI (though in the words of the 2013 CPI, it 'measures the perceived levels of public sector corruption'), thus reflecting the general confusion.

1. B2B: some prefer a broad definition of corruption.

Unfortunately, even TI's first—narrow—definition is subject to diverse interpretations. Is the 'abuse of public office' limited to essentially *economic* improprieties—sometimes described as 'modern' corruption—such as embezzlement or accepting bribes? Or does it include what are sometimes called *social* improprieties—or 'traditional' corruption—such as appointing members of one's family (nepotism) or friends and colleagues (cronyism) to public office when they are not the best-qualified person for the post? Do political parties, especially those not represented in the legislature, hold public office—and, if not, can they be accused of corruption in this narrow sense?

Another problem with the term 'public office' has become more pronounced in recent decades as neo-liberalism has spread across the globe. Neo-liberalism is an ideology that advocates a reduction in the role of the state and an enhanced role for the market. One of its key features is that it blurs 'public' and 'private'. Many states now outsource tasks they once performed themselves, but which the public still considers to be the state's responsibility. For instance, prisons were once run almost exclusively by the state, whereas an increasing number nowadays are run by private companies under contract to the state. If a prison warder employed by a private company accepts bribes to smuggle drugs into prisons for use by inmates, is s/he being corrupt according to the narrow definition? Is such a person occupying a *private* or a *public* office? Our view is that if citizens consider a given office as ultimately the state's responsibility, then someone abusing that office for personal or group advantage is corrupt.

The term 'private gain' is also far from straightforward. There is universal agreement that a state functionary who accepts bribes for personal enrichment is being corrupt. But what about office-holders of political parties who accept questionable donations for their organization, but who appear to derive no immediate *personal* benefit? This is a less clear-cut example than the first, and is subject to different opinions.

It should by now be clear that there are often perfectly good reasons for differences both in defining corruption generally, and in deciding whether a particular act or failure to act (omission) constitutes corruption. We can now explore the reasons for such differences.

Reasons for different conceptions of corruption

One reason for different interpretations of corruption is culture. Here, culture can be defined as the dominant beliefs, attitudes, and behaviour in a given society, which might relate to its principal religion, and whether or not the country was a colony or a colonial power. In short, culture is heavily influenced by tradition and history.

An example of a cultural interpretation of differing approaches to corruption is that what was earlier described as 'economic' or 'modern' corruption has been called 'Western' corruption, whereas 'social' or 'traditional' corruption has been labelled 'Asiatic'. Like so many labels in social science, there are problems with these two, and they can be very misleading. For instance, some argue that patronage and clientelism are typical of Asian societies, where they are—allegedly—not seen as forms of corruption. There are at least two major problems with this claim.

First, dominant views on whether or not patronage and clientelism constitute corruption vary across Asia; they are not the same in Singapore as in Cambodia, for example. Views on these vary in 'the West' too. Whereas most Anglophone and Nordic specialists on corruption maintain that clientelism constitutes a form of corruption, most Italian specialists reject this. In fact, opinion surveys in various countries reveal that even the notion of 'dominant views' of what constitutes corruption is often misleading. In the late 1990s and early 2000s, the World Bank conducted 'diagnostic surveys' in various countries. These included imaginary scenarios, and respondents were asked whether or not they considered them to be examples of corruption; in many cases, it emerged that respondents' views were deeply divided. So the assumption that 'Russians' or 'the British' have a common understanding of corruption is challenged by survey results. Moreover, it should not be assumed that just because government spokespersons from Country X claim 'this is not corruption, it is simply part of our culture', most citizens agree with this. Again, surveys reveal that many citizens *do* consider a given activity corrupt, and do not condone it; but they feel helpless to challenge their elites, who maintain that it is part of their culture purely in order to justify their own questionable behaviour. The second—even more persuasive—counter-argument is that there is plenty of 'traditional' corruption in the West, and no shortage of 'modern' corruption in Asia.

We can now consider an example of what is often seen as a cultural difference between four countries in terms of their attitudes towards personal ties. The four terms examined are the Russian concept of *blat*, the Chinese concept of *guanxi*, the originally American (though increasingly globalized) concept of networking, and the British—primarily English—concept of the 'old school tie'.

The Russian term has been changing its meaning in recent years, but in Soviet times referred to informal agreements between people to help each other through non-monetary exchange; it is thus close to the concept of bartering, and was a coping mechanism in a system in which there were widespread shortages of both durable and non-durable consumer goods. Thus, a farmer might have agreed with an electrician to supply the latter with eggs and chickens for two years in return for having his old farmhouse re-wired. But whereas bartering is merely a form of exchange between people, *blat* involves the development of personal relations, notably trust and a sense of reciprocity, between those engaged in it.

The Chinese concept of *guanxi* also refers to relationships that develop between individuals or groups, and that involve potentially long-term mutual obligations—reciprocity. I might develop either a friendship or a professional relationship with a Chinese person, whom I help in some way. That person then feels obliged to return the favour at some point in the future, perhaps many years later. But he or she will not forget that I am owed a favour.

The increasingly popular notion of networking involves the creation of informal ties intended to bring benefit to those involved. If I cultivate someone I meet at a business convention or an academic conference with the ultimate aim of taking advantage of that contact, I am attempting to influence that person on the basis of a (possibly weakly developed) relationship, rather than purely in terms of my qualifications. Hence, while this is probably the least criticized of the four types of informal relationship analysed here, it can still be seen as a form of corruption if a very broad definition of that term is adopted.

Whereas many would reject the notion that networking has anything in common with corruption, the British concept of the 'old school tie' is widely criticized. People who may not even have met nevertheless privilege each other on the basis of having attended an elite group of schools in the UK. Thus, A, B, and C all attended leading public (i.e. the most elitist private) schools. C is seeking employment, and is known to B, who encourages A—who has never met C—to offer C a position, even though C is not the best qualified person for that position. Of the four types of informal relationships considered here, the 'old school tie' is the most exclusionary; if I did not attend one of the elite schools as a child, there is no way I can ever break into the insider group. This is an important distinction between the first three types of relationship and this one, which is the most open to classification as a form of corruption.

The main point to note about these four versions of informal ties is that, while each is distinct and culturally specific, there are also commonalities between them. All four involve the creation of insiders and outsiders, with privileges for the insiders. All four are seen by some members of society as corrupt, though a far higher proportion of Britons would consider the 'old school tie' as improper than Chinese would criticize *guanxi* or Americans would question networking. In short, cultural differences exist, but are often exaggerated.

Of course, if the narrow version of corruption is adopted, none of these would constitute corruption unless the relationship involved an officer of the state. But adopting the broad version leaves the door wide open to describe all sorts of relationships between people—even friendships—as corrupt; this is one of the principal reasons why the preference in this study is for the narrower approach to defining corruption.

In addition to cultural factors, another problem arises because different jurisdictions work to different definitions of corruption. While this may partly be explained by and linked to cultural differences, there are other reasons. The main one is that the legislative situation varies. This can be because legislators have been advised by different specialists. In more open and democratic societies, legislation may be the result of compromise between different groups both within and beyond parliament—and the particular permutation of diverse interests is unique to each society. This explanation is less likely to apply in authoritarian systems. But such systems are typically more corrupt than more democratic ones, and ruling elites often choose either to have no explicit anti-corruption legislation—and hence no legal definition—or else deliberately vague laws; they want to preserve their privileged positions, and prefer not to introduce laws that could be used to undermine these.

Finally, analysts sometimes choose narrow definitions of corruption for methodological reasons. Thus, a leading German scholar opted to define corruption principally as bribery for one of his analyses, since it was more straightforward to conceptualize it in this way than to include more disputed aspects such as social corruption.

Classifications of corruption

Before elaborating the dominant approach to corruption used in this book, it is worth considering some of the ways in which analysts have classified different types of corruption.

In line with the point that the views of most citizens might differ from those of the elites, the scholar often seen as the grandfather of comparative corruption studies, Arnold Heidenheimer, drew a useful distinction between what he called 'black', 'white', and 'gray' (using US spelling) corruption. Based on his awareness that elites and ordinary citizens sometimes perceive phenomena in different ways, Heidenheimer defined black corruption as activities that most members of both the elites and the masses condemn and want to see punished, whereas white corruption refers to activities that, while still formally perceived as corruption, are more or less tolerated by both groups, who do not want to see perpetrators penalized. Gray corruption refers to activities about which elites and the general public have differing views, or about which there are significant differences of opinion, including ambivalence, even within each of these two main groups.

Another tripartite distinction drawn by Heidenheimer is between public office-centred, market-centred, and public interest-centred approaches to corruption. The first focuses on corruption as behaviour that deviates from that expected of a public official, and that is explained in terms of the official's desire for improper personal benefit. Market-centred approaches interpret corruption in terms of public officials treating their positions as a source of private income or business. What they can offer and what they can charge (e.g. how much they can demand as a bribe) depends on the supply of and demand for the good or service they are offering—in short, on the market situation. Finally, the public interest-centred approach focuses on the harm done to the public because of the improper self-serving behaviour of public officials.

A third distinction often drawn is between 'grass-eating' and 'meat-eating' corruption. These terms were coined in the Knapp Commission's early-1970s report on corruption in the New York Police Department. The former refers to officials who will accept a bribe if offered one, whereas the latter refers to more predatory corruption, in which officials actually solicit bribes; the former is also sometimes called reactive corruption, and the latter proactive. A related approach is to distinguish between extortive and transactive corruption. In the former, the bribe-taker exerts pressure on someone to give a bribe, which basically equates to meat-eating. In the latter, the two agents (bribe- or favour-taker and bribe- or favour-giver) are more equal; both are basically willing partners, who negotiate a deal.

A distinction found in many official anti-corruption documents might initially appear to refer to the same phenomena as 'grass-eating' and 'meat-eating' corruption, since 'passive' looks like an alternative way of describing the former, and 'active' as another term for the latter. But this is not how the terms are used. The first typically describes the act of offering a bribe, whereas the second refers to acceptance of a bribe. This usage is problematic, since the connotations of the terms active and passive in such an application suggest that the recipient of the bribe—an official—is less responsible for the improper act than the so-called donor. Thus, a police officer who suggests to a motorist that a bribe would ensure the non-issuance of a speeding fine would, in this classification, be described as passively corrupt, whereas the motorist would be actively corrupt. While the use of these terms is arguably more acceptable if applied, for instance, to a corporation that exerts pressure on a previously uncorrupt procurement officer to accept a bribe, it is highly misleading in cases where an officer of the state extorts money from a citizen or business. Moreover, if it is accepted that officers of the state should be setting an example to ordinary citizens and even the business sector, it becomes clear why this terminology is confusing.

A fifth distinction is between petty (or low level) and grand (high level or elite) corruption. The former applies to the kinds of corruption the ordinary citizen is likely to encounter in their everyday lives—while driving, or applying for a permit to extend their house, for example. Grand corruption, as its name suggests, refers to corruption at the elite level, such as politicians adopting legislation that favours a group that has bribed them, or a minister giving the go-ahead for a major development against the recommendations of her advisers and even the regulations—again in return for a bribe. If the broad definition of corruption (i.e. including self-interested misconduct solely within the private sector) is included, much corruption would be at the level of the corporation and thus closer to grand corruption.

Along somewhat similar lines, the World Bank has since 2000 distinguished between 'administrative (or bureaucratic) corruption' and 'state capture'. The latter has been described by Joel Hellman and Daniel Kaufmann, both at the time working for the World Bank, as '*a form* of grand corruption' (emphasis added); in 2000, together with Geraint Jones (also of the World Bank), they defined state capture as:

> firms shaping and affecting *formulation* of the rules of the game through private payments to public officials and politicians (emphasis added)

Since the original coining of the term, its usage has been broadened by other analysts to include, for instance, improper efforts by organized crime to influence legislation. Hellman, Jones, and Kaufmann defined 'administrative corruption' as:

> 'petty' forms of bribery in connection with the *implementation* of laws, rules, and regulations (emphasis added)

Many analysts have since broadened the usage of this term too, so that any improper actions or omissions relating to the implementation of rules can be described as administrative corruption.

As with the terms 'active' and 'passive' corruption, a drawback of the term 'state capture' is that it can be interpreted to imply that those offering bribes are more culpable than those accepting them. The World Bank officials who originally promoted the concepts stress that this is not their intention; they are particularly concerned with the officers of the state who accept the bribes. But the potential for misunderstanding would have been reduced had a term that focused attention on the corrupt officials—such as 'selling the state' instead of 'state capture'—been adopted.

A more complex typology than the World Bank's has been produced by Rasma Karklins. Focusing mainly on the post-communist transition states (here meaning in transition from one kind of authoritarianism to either democracy or another kind of authoritarianism) of Central and Eastern Europe (CEE), she divides corrupt acts into three basic types, each of which is further sub-divided—low-level administrative corruption; self-serving asset-stripping by officials; and state capture by corrupt networks. Types one and three are basically the same as the World Bank's. But Karklins' second one is an important addition, and can be found in many transition countries in recent years. Thus, analysts of the post-communist states often refer to '*nomenklatura privatization*'. This was a process common in many CEE countries during the 1990s, in which the former elites from the Communist era—the *nomenklatura*—were able to take ethically questionable advantage in various ways (e.g. kickbacks from purchasers; direct purchase themselves at knock-down prices) of the sell-off of previously state-owned enterprises.

Related concepts

Many phenomena overlap with, or are similar to, corruption. Since corruption itself is a disputed concept and can be interpreted in both narrow and broad ways, it follows that some will distinguish between closely related concepts, whereas others will want to see them as variants of corruption. Bearing this in mind, the following distinctions introduce readers to the main terms often seen as related to corruption.

Bribery and Corruption

The fact that we talk in English of 'bribery and corruption' in itself implies their close connection. But, as became clear from the earlier discussion of social corruption, corruption can be in the form of improper professional relationships—favouritism of one kind or another—and thus need not involve bribery. Moreover, some officials take advantage of their position to embezzle funds from the state; this is another form of corruption that does not involve bribery. Conversely, bribery can occur purely within the private sector; while this constitutes corruption in its broad sense, it is not corruption in its narrow sense.

Bribes and gifts

One of the trickiest issues in determining whether or not a given act constitutes corruption is how to distinguish a gift from a bribe. In many Asian cultures, not only is a gift not seen as a bribe, but it can be insulting to decline it, or to treat it as essentially a bribe. This is an example of cultural difference; not only elites, but also most citizens in most Asian states believe that it is polite and required to show hospitality by giving a visitor a gift. Conversely, many Westerners have reservations about accepting gifts. As so often applies in attempting to determine appropriate boundaries for corruption, this issue cannot be seen in simple black and white terms. Moreover, Westerners are sometimes unwittingly hypocritical on this issue; many managers who criticize or feel uncomfortable about Asian 'gift-giving' consider it appropriate to give their personal assistants presents at Christmas as a way of showing their appreciation for the assistants' hard work and loyalty over the previous year.

While there can be no definitive solution to this issue, we can in most cases distinguish reasonably clearly between a gift and a bribe by considering a list of six variables:

1. *The intention of the donor.* Does the person offering the 'gift' either implicitly or explicitly expect something in return? If not, the term bribe—and hence the possibility of corruption—does not apply.

2. *The expectation of the recipient.* Does the person receiving the 'gift' expect to have to reciprocate in some way? If not, the receiving of a gift is much less likely to constitute an act of corruption.

3. *The timing of the giving.* If a supplicant—someone who, for example, wants to secure a permit to construct a new tower block—offers a 'gift' to the relevant official *before* that official has reached a decision, it almost certainly constitutes a bribe. If the gift is offered *after* a final decision has been made and there was no earlier hint from the supplicant that a positive outcome on the application might result in a reward, then the gift is less likely to constitute a bribe.

4. *Value of the 'gift'.* Obviously, giving a teacher an apple is very different from giving her a new Mercedes-Benz. In fact, the difference is of degree, rather than a qualitative one. However, an increasing number of states and international organizations now recognize that the difference of degree is so great that a distinction should be drawn between the two acts. Where to draw the line can be problematic, however; this issue is revisited in Chapter 6.

5. *The legal perspective.* This is a formal variable, and involves examining what the laws or regulations proscribe in a given country or organization. For instance, police officers in Singapore are prohibited from accepting free drinks from fast-food outlets, whereas in parts of Australia, there is no such regulation. This variable differs from the other five in that it can be removed from this list without affecting the latter's utility.

6. *The perceived social acceptability of the transaction.* Unlike the previous variable, this one focuses on informal dimensions of the issue, namely the views of most members of the public. It has been noted that cultures can have different views on what constitutes corruption and its level of acceptability. One way of acknowledging such differences is to seek to determine the dominant attitudes towards a given act or omission in each country through surveys, analysis of the media, etc.

Corporate and white-collar crime

It will be recalled that TI changed its preferred definition in 2000 to allow for the fact that corruption could, in their view, occur purely within the private sector (B2B corruption). However, this approach stretches the concept of corruption unnecessarily, and there are good reasons for distinguishing between the state and the private sector. In most cases, if I am dissatisfied with the goods or services of one private company, I can switch my custom to another; market economics is based on competition. But the state has a virtual monopoly; if I do not trust the judiciary or police, for instance, I cannot turn elsewhere for law enforcement. Moreover, in cases of disagreement, the state should be an arbiter—a referee—between individuals and organizations; the business sector does not perform the same role. These are two good reasons why it makes sense to distinguish the state from the private sector.

Finally, there are perfectly adequate terms to describe abuse of one's position for personal gain in the private sector or malfeasant behaviour by private organizations. The most common term for the former is white-collar crime, while corporate crime is widely used to describe the latter. A major drawback of both terms is that much of what is reported in the media as 'crime' is not in fact illegal, merely socially unacceptable (i.e. illicit rather than illegal). It is therefore usually preferable to label them respectively white-collar misconduct and corporate misconduct, although it is appropriate to call particular cases crimes if the law has been broken.

Organized crime

There is often considerable overlap and interaction between organized crime and corruption; indeed, organized crime could not get away with as much as it does were it not for collusion between criminal organizations and corrupt officials. There are also many similarities between the two phenomena. Both criminal gangs and corrupt officials pursue vested interests that run counter to those of society and the state. Both organized crime and corruption can involve activities considered improper by most citizens but that are not technically illegal (so that organized *crime* is not invariably an accurate term for the activities of some gangs). While some analysts distinguish organized crime from corruption by arguing that the former necessarily involves violence (whether actual or threatened) whereas the latter does not, police officers sometimes use or threaten violence in a way not sanctioned by the state.

But a key conceptual difference is that corruption involves officials (or private-sector executives and professionals, if the broad definition of corruption is used), whereas organized crime does not, unless collusion is involved. Another is that corrupt officials sometimes operate on an individual basis—as so-called rotten apples—whereas organized crime necessarily involves group activity.

An alternative to definitions

For most situations, the narrow definition used by the World Bank and so many other organizations and specialists is adequate, if not totally unproblematic. But when a more nuanced or detailed approach is required, we can use five criteria to identify an action or omission (e.g. deliberately turning a blind eye in return for some reward) as corrupt or not; all five must be met for the action or omission to constitute corruption (see Box 1).

This set of criteria conforms to our own preference for the narrow definition of corruption. But it can easily be modified—by substituting 'a position of entrusted power' for 'public office', for instance—to suit those who prefer the broad definition. In the remainder of this book, while the emphasis is on official (narrow) corruption, examples from the corporate world and even sport will also be cited.

It has been shown that there is no universal agreement on what constitutes corruption, and why this is so. Nevertheless, there is

Box 1 Criteria for identifying corruption

- the action or omission must involve an individual or a group occupying public office, whether elected or appointed

- the public office must involve a degree of authority relating to decision-making powers, law enforcement, or defence of the state

- the officials must commit the act or omit to do what they should at least partly because of personal interests or the interests of an organization to which they belong (e.g. a political party) or both, and these interests must ultimately run counter to those of the state and society

- the officials act or omit to act partly or wholly in a clandestine manner, and are aware that their behaviour is or might be considered illegal or illicit. If uncertain about the level of impropriety, the officials opt not to check this—not to subject their actions to the so-called *sunlight test* (i.e. permitting open scrutiny of their actions)—because they wish to maximize their own interests

- the action or omission must be perceived by a significant proportion of the population and/or the state as corrupt. This final criterion helps to overcome the problem of cultural difference in interpreting corruption

widespread agreement on the narrow definition—private abuse of public office—as a starting point, even if the terms private abuse and public office are subject to interpretation. Applying the five criteria test will in most cases satisfactorily answer the question of whether or not a particular action or omission constitutes corruption, and will be used for the rest of this book. Beyond that test, individuals must decide for themselves on the basis of the so-called elephant test—'it is difficult to describe, but I know it when I see it'—whether or not a particular case constitutes corruption.

Chapter 2
Why corruption is a problem

Corruption impacts upon individuals, groups and organizations (including the state) in numerous ways. While many of its negative effects are obvious, others are less so. For the sake of a clearer exposition, they are considered here in terms of social, environmental, economic, politico-legal, security-related, and international implications; in the real world, the impact of particular acts of corruption is often on several areas simultaneously.

Society

There are so many ways in which corruption can negatively impact on society that selectivity is required here. One is on the working and living conditions of ordinary people. In a speech delivered in Washington DC in May 2013, the Executive Director of the Ugandan Anti-Corruption Coalition argued that if the vast sum corruptly diverted from government pension funds in a scandal that broke in her country in 2012 had been properly invested, it could have resulted in a well-needed salary boost of 50 per cent for more than 30,000 primary school teachers or 46,000 police constables, or it could have provided almost 18 million doses of anti-malaria therapy.

For many developing and transition states, one of the most serious problems of corruption is that it can result in reduced aid, as potential donors or lenders either terminate or refuse to provide funds to countries in which elites appear to be diverting most of these resources for personal gain. Unfortunately, it is usually the poorest members of society who suffer most from this.

Corruption tends to create a greater sense of 'them' and 'us' in society, both vertically and horizontally. The gap between elites and the public is often wider than necessary because corrupt officials are perceived to be creaming off a country's wealth at the expense of ordinary citizens (i.e. a vertical divide). At the same time, corruption can increase divisions between citizens themselves (horizontal divide), as those unwilling or unable to pay bribes to obtain what they need become resentful of those who can and do.

A related fact is that corruption can increase inequality. While many citizens will tolerate reasonably high levels of inequality if this appears to be based on merit, they will resent it if based more on personal connections and bribery to obtain prestigious jobs and promotions. The problem is exacerbated if growing inequality is accompanied by higher levels of poverty, which is often the case. In a seminal analysis published by the IMF in 1998, the authors analyse data from more than thirty countries over an 18-year period and demonstrate convincingly that increased levels of corruption increase both income inequality (as reflected in the Gini coefficient) and poverty levels. Since poverty is linked to poorer health, both physical and mental, corruption can impact directly on people's well-being.

If corruption means increased distrust of the state and its officers, there can be a widespread 'return to the family' and increased attachment to kinship. A potentially negative effect of this is that enhanced identification with 'kith and kin' can result in reduced social capital and growing estrangement between groups in society, which can lead to ethnic conflict.

High levels of corruption and the consequent low levels of trust in the state can increase the sense of insecurity in society. For example, if citizens do not trust their law enforcement officers because of the latters' corruption, they will be less willing to report crimes to the authorities and to cooperate with those authorities; this typically leads to higher crime rates, and hence a greater sense of insecurity among the general public.

Officials themselves can feel more insecure because of corruption. If the political elite decides to clamp down heavily on corruption, even honest officials may be concerned that actions not currently seen as corrupt may in the future be classified as such, with the concomitant penalties; this can lead them to hesitate in fulfilling their normal and proper duties, or even to refuse altogether to perform them. In an ideal rule-of-law state, in which no legislation is ever retrospective, this problem would not arise; but few states nowadays, even in the West, adhere strictly to the notion of no retroactive laws.

In many post-communist countries, the early transition phase was rendered more difficult because these states had for decades had no true capitalist class, and hence no group with legitimate funds to invest in the new marketized and privatized economy. In such a situation, corruption can help to create a new wealthy bourgeoisie; but this is based on illicit income, which undermines popular support for this new class and its ideas.

According to some analysts, the joint (with cybercrime) fastest growing branch of organized crime in recent years is human trafficking. The scale of such trafficking is significantly higher than it would otherwise be because of the collusion of corrupt officials in this modern form of slavery. One of the main African countries from which many women are trafficked into Europe for prostitution purposes is Nigeria: Osita Agbu has provided a detailed analysis of the role of corrupt officials in this.

In addition to the role of corruption in human trafficking, corrupt officials can be complicit in arms trafficking, which can increase homicide rates and aid terrorists. Two Bangladeshi government ministers were sentenced to death in 2014 for their involvement in weapons trafficking.

Corruption can endanger lives. This assumes various forms, one of which relates to flooding. Among the many advantages trees have is that they can bind soil; but in some countries, corrupt officials have on occasions turned a blind eye to the logging of trees along riverbanks in return for bribes. This has sometimes resulted in riverbanks collapsing following heavy rains, with the destruction of thousands of properties built at the water's edge, and many lives lost in the floods.

Another all too common way in which corruption can endanger lives relates to the construction industry. Building and safety inspectors who ignore malpractice in this industry, including the use of sub-standard materials, in return for bribes have been prosecuted for injuries and even deaths arising from improper construction work. A particularly serious example, in which thirty-five people were killed, was of a building collapse in the Egyptian city of Alexandria in 2007, which led to allegations of widespread corruption among local officials. Clearly the Egyptian authorities need to do far more, with further examples from this and other cities occurring more recently; at least twenty-four people were killed in January 2013 when their apartment block in Alexandria collapsed—again resulting in serious allegations of corruption, including from the Minister of Housing (Figure 2). In terms of the number of people killed, even worse was the collapse of a department store in Seoul (South Korea) in 1995 that resulted in 502 deaths; the collapse was eventually attributed partly to the corruption of two city building inspectors, who were found guilty of accepting bribes during the building's construction phase.

2. A building in Egypt collapses in 2012, killing 19, allegedly as a result of corruption.

China is another country that has experienced such problems. In 2009, the Chinese authorities acknowledged that more than 5,000 schoolchildren had died in the previous year's earthquake in Sichuan, following complaints that many of the deaths had been caused by the collapse of school buildings that were sub-standard as a result of corruption. Following the collapse in 2009 of a 13-storey building under construction in Shanghai that killed a building worker, the editor of state-run newspaper *China Daily* complained about the 'often corrupt nexus between Chinese property developers and local government officials who depend on property taxes and land sales for a significant proportion of their income'.

The focus so far has been on the negative impact of corruption in the narrow sense (i.e. that involves state officials). But in the 21st century, the general public has become far more aware of the potentially devastating effects of corruption in its broad sense. As one Western corporation after another—Enron (USA),

Worldcom (USA), Parmalat (Italy), Siemens (Germany), AWB (Australia), to name just a few—has been shown to have been engaging in misconduct, including bribery and kickbacks to secure overseas contracts, so the public's trust in the corporate sector has plummeted. Many maintain that the 2008 Global Financial Crisis was partly the result of corporate misconduct, and have cited this as the source of major economic problems that have had such a deleterious social impact, including on employment and pension schemes.

The *reporting* of corruption can also have a negative effect on the public, since it can increase a general sense of disappointment, even despair. Finding the optimal amount and type of reporting is difficult, however; to cite a truism, 'bad news is good news' for the media, and few can restrain themselves from reporting as many scandals as they can, whether or not allegations have been thoroughly investigated. Irresponsible reporting of corruption can make people suspicious of the 'watchdog' role of the media, which has negative implications for the development of civil society.

Environment

Arguably the greatest long-term issue facing humanity is the environment. Unfortunately, corruption generally compounds the already existing problems in this area. According to the United Nations Office on Drugs and Crime (UNODC), environment-related corruption includes:

> Such practices (as) embezzlement during the implementation of environmental programmes, grand corruption in the issuance of permits and licenses for natural resources exploitation, and petty bribery of law enforcers.

The UNODC has also identified sectors most at risk: they include forestry, oil exploitation, the trafficking of endangered species, and hazardous waste management.

Many of the world's largest producers and exporters of timber, including Brazil, Indonesia, and Russia, have experienced substantial environmental damage because of illegal logging facilitated by corrupt officials. There are claims that more than half the timber produced in the world in recent years is the result of such logging, much of it involving bribery and corruption.

As for endangered species—in 2011, the head of the 'Freeland' NGO that seeks to combat wildlife trafficking argued vis-à-vis South-East Asia that the number one problem his organization was running into with its anti-trafficking programme was corruption, especially high-level corruption. Corruption can contribute to the extinction of various species of wildlife.

Economy

The most researched and reported aspect of the impact of corruption is the economic. In an oft-cited analysis published in the mid-1990s, economist Paolo Mauro argued against those who had in the 1960s claimed that corruption—for instance, in the form of facilitation payments or 'speed money' to state bureaucrats to accelerate the issuance of permits—could actually increase economic growth rates. On the basis of a considerable amount of data, he compared growth rates with subjective assessments of the level of corruption in various countries, and concluded that corruption discouraged investment, which in turn decreased growth rates. While some have challenged this argument, the majority view is that Mauro was basically correct. For instance, in an article published in 2000, Shang-Jin Wei argued that foreign direct investment (FDI) is lower in countries with higher rates of corruption, as potential investors are deterred by it.

Perceptions of high levels of corruption in a given country can render it either difficult or impossible for that country to be admitted to international 'clubs'—notably the EU—that it is hoping to join precisely because it sees substantial potential economic benefits in such membership. Even once in such supra-national groupings, perceived high levels of corruption can have serious economic repercussions: Bulgaria, Romania, and Czechia are three relatively new members of the EU (the first two since 2007, the third since 2004) that have suffered major funding cuts from the EU since joining precisely because of the latter's concerns about their corruption levels. In addition, both Bulgaria and Romania were blocked in their attempts to join the Schengen zone (an area comprising twenty-six European countries, between which there are no border controls) because some West European EU member-states—notably Germany and the Netherlands—were concerned that these South-East European countries had excessively porous frontiers with their non-EU neighbours, largely because of high levels of corruption among border guards and customs officers.

A serious economic problem the EU itself has experienced has been partly blamed on corruption. A 2012 TI report entitled *Money, Politics, Power—Corruption Risks in Europe* identified corruption in several EU states (with Greece being seen as a major culprit) as a significant factor in the emergence of the Eurozone crisis that erupted in 2010.

Corruption leads to decreased revenue to the state, as corrupt officials exempt citizens and firms from fines, taxes, etc. in return for bribes. In the EU's first ever anti-corruption report, published in February 2014, it was claimed that corruption costs EU states collectively some 120 billion Euros a year. This was a rather similar amount to the sum (US$150 billion) the African Union estimated in 2002 was lost each year to corruption among its fifty-three member states—though the EU figure, while substantial, did not account for approximately one quarter of the total GDP of the region as the sub-Saharan African one did.

Several states, mostly transition ones, have in recent years introduced flat-rate income and corporate tax systems, often precisely to reduce the risk of lost state revenue. The rationale is that progressive tax systems involve more discretionary decision-making by tax officials, and hence provide more corruption opportunities, than flat-rate systems; both individuals and companies can declare lower income in progressive tax systems than they actually receive, so as to be taxed in a lower tax bracket (i.e. a form of tax evasion). Unfortunately, flat-rate systems are not watertight either, since individuals and firms can still collude with corrupt officials to report less taxable income than they should, thus depriving the state of legitimate revenue.

Corruption can result in reduced economic competition, as corrupt officials favour firms that pay them bribes—for example, to give them unfair preferential treatment in acquiring factories that a state is privatizing, or to secure contracts from the state. Reduced competition typically leads to higher prices and costs, as well as less choice, all of which are detrimental to both consumers and the state itself.

A factor with potentially serious negative economic ramifications for the development and well-being of a country is that social corruption (nepotism, cronyism, etc.) can discourage honest, well-qualified people, who become frustrated at not securing good positions or being promoted. Some simply stop working hard and using their initiative, while others emigrate to a less corrupt and more meritocratic country. Corruption can thus encourage a brain drain, depriving society of the people best suited to run the country and its economy. This phenomenon, sometimes called human capital flight, has been a particularly acute problem for countries such as Iran.

But conventional capital flight is also a corruption-related problem. Shortly after becoming President of Russia for the first time, in July 2000, Vladimir Putin convened a meeting of many of Russia's wealthiest individuals, the so-called oligarchs, at which he informed them that he would not scrutinize the origins of their fortunes as long as they abided by four rules; one was that they repatriate the considerable sums they had sent overseas. While it is a moot point whether or not most oligarchs should be labelled corrupt, the meeting is noteworthy for clearly revealing the senior leadership's concern about capital flight. This has been a problem for many other states in recent years, and corrupt officials at all levels, including the highest, are a major source of the problem.

It is not only the public and the state that can suffer economically from corruption. Corporations that bribe officials to secure contracts are sometimes exposed, with serious negative consequences. In 2013, the Independent Commission Against Corruption (ICAC) in the Australian state of New South Wales (NSW) deemed certain mining licences in the Hunter Valley to have been corruptly acquired. In light of this, the NSW government announced in January 2014 that the licences were being revoked.

Political and legal system

Corruption can negatively affect political systems (e.g. democracies or autocracies) and regimes (the team running the system) in numerous ways. For example, it can unfairly increase the power and influence of individual legislators willing to privilege whoever is prepared to pay them bribes or enhance their prospects in future elections. The latter is seen around the world in the form of pork-barrelling, whereby legislators inappropriately allocate or promise funds to particular constituencies so as to increase voter support.

However, this point about inappropriate favouritism leads us to a particularly grey area in corruption studies, the issue of lobbying. In countries such as the USA, lobbying is legal and formally organized. But some see lobbying as a form of corruption, and have argued that it is essentially a functional equivalent in wealthy states of the more clearly corrupt attempts to influence politicians in poorer countries (see the reference to 'state capture' in Chapter 1). But in deciding whether or not lobbying constitutes a form of corruption, it is necessary to examine the precise nature of specific cases; generalization can be misleading.

Many organizations lobby for causes that most people would consider perfectly legitimate, such as the World Wildlife Fund or other charity organizations, and such lobbying should be distinguished from that relating to more obviously vested interests. Moreover, if the funding of lobbying is of officially registered agencies rather than for paying bribes, and if—and this is an important caveat—the financial details of such agencies are fully transparent, then it would be inappropriate to label this corruption. Lobbying by some types of organization might seem unfair, giving those with sufficient resources better opportunities than are available to the average person to attempt to influence political decision-makers, but it is only another aspect of the political inequality that exists in even the most democratic systems. It is thus as much a problem for theorists of democracy as for analysts of corruption.

Another tricky issue for both theorists and practitioners of democracy is how best to fund political parties—in particular, whether or not this can be done in a corruption-proof way. In 1999, Germany witnessed the emergence of the so-called Kohlgate scandal, in which honorary chair of the Christian Democratic Union (CDU) Helmut Kohl was accused of being involved in the corrupt acceptance and distribution of illicit funds for his party during his term as Chancellor (prime minister) of Germany (1982–98). The CDU was eventually found guilty of corruption, and the President of the lower house of parliament sought to fine the party a total of just under 50 million marks (approximately 25 million Euros). Although this penalty was eventually quashed, German party financing rules were substantially amended—rendered more transparent and less dependent on business contributions—as a direct result of the Kohlgate affair. The particular significance of this case was less the fact that a

leading Western politician had been accused of corruption—
France's Jacques Chirac and Italy's Silvio Berlusconi have also
faced charges of corruption in recent years—but that it happened
in a country reputed to have one of the best party financing
systems in the world.

Corruption can undermine electoral competition, increasing
inequalities between political parties, and reducing party
competitiveness. Electoral fraud and impropriety assumes
many forms; two of the most common are ballot-rigging and
vote-buying (see Figure 3). There have been innumerable alleged
and proven cases of both in most parts of the world in recent
years. But, as with so many forms of corruption, neither is either a
new phenomenon or unique to developing and transition states:
an early example of vote-buying is the 1768 'spendthrift election'
in Northamptonshire (UK).

Citizen despair can increase the attractiveness to voters of extremist
politicians, whether of the left or the right, who promise to eradicate

3. Ballot-rigging is still all too common in many countries.

corruption. Empirical research indicates that such extremists generally prove to be ineffectual at reducing corruption if elected; but there is a widespread belief in some countries that they have a magic bullet.

Accusations of corruption by one party or politician can attract counter-accusations. This can result in increased dissatisfaction among voters, with various undesirable outcomes. One is that citizens become cynical, and therefore alienated from the political system, albeit in a passive way. Another is that they become incensed, leading to active mass unrest that delegitimizes and destabilizes the system and can lead to the overthrow of the regime, or even the system itself. In his 2012 analysis of corruption, Frank Vogl focuses on the so-called Arab Spring of 2011, and sees public anger at corruption as a major factor in the collapse of the regimes and systems in Egypt and Tunisia.

Thus corruption can undermine system legitimacy—the perceived right of the rulers to rule. Too much corruption and its reporting can result in people losing faith in the market, democracy, and the rule of law. While this tends to be more destabilizing in transition states, the point applies even to developed Western states. In January 2013, the Secretary General of the Council of Europe argued that 'Corruption is the biggest single threat to democracy in Europe today. More and more people on our continent are losing faith in the rule of law.'

If people lose faith in the rule of law in states where it has previously existed, the likelihood of arbitrary abuse of civil liberties and human rights increases. While this problem initially affects ordinary citizens, excessive arbitrariness can be dangerous to political elites too, as their rule is threatened by mass unrest. Like so many other aspects of corruption, this danger is nothing new; in East Asia's traditional concept of the 'mandate of heaven', the people had the right to remove an emperor who was inept, tyrannical, or corrupt.

Security

For a state to exercise its defence, law enforcement, and welfare functions properly it needs adequate funding; if corruption reduces government revenue, this has detrimental effects on the state's overall capacity to protect the populace. There is a strong correlation between weak states and high levels of corruption.

During the 1990s, when security at military bases in many Soviet successor states was frighteningly lax, various Western government reports and academic analyses claimed that corrupt officials in Russia and Ukraine were illegally selling nuclear materials to whoever would pay them. While much of the evidence on this is circumstantial, there is irrefutable proof that corrupt officials in weak states have sold various kinds of weapons to organized crime gangs and terrorists.

But this point can apply to mature democracies too. In March 2014, as a result of an FBI sting operation, a Californian state senator was arrested and charged with colluding with US-based Chinese organized crime in trafficking weapons to an Islamic rebel group based in the Philippines: the senator's pay-off, according to the FBI, was donations to his political campaign. He was allegedly planning to expand his trafficking operation into Africa, and was indifferent to the harm his trafficking might cause; the case was ongoing at the time of writing.

A final point about mature democracies and arms dealing is that a number of Western corporations have been accused of paying substantial bribes to overseas government officials to secure contracts for the purchase of military equipment; it is not only individuals and gangs that are corruptly involved in this potentially deadly business.

International

Some of the effects of corruption in one country on other countries are irritating rather than a real danger. For instance, car insurance premiums in Germany increased in the 1990s partly because so many cars were being stolen there and smuggled to Central and East European states; this racket often involved gangs bribing customs officials to look the other way while the cars were in transit.

But many international ramifications of corruption are far more serious. For instance, criminal organizations involved in international trafficking—including of drugs, weapons, humans, and human parts—would be far less effective were it not for the fact that they can often bribe customs officers, police officers, and other officials to turn a blind eye to their activities, or to warn them in advance of impending raids (e.g. of illegal brothels in which there are transnationally trafficked persons).

Unfortunately, pragmatism often dominates principle in international relations, and countries that appear to have relatively low levels of corruption may *de facto* tolerate high levels of corruption in a country that has nuclear weapons or commodities (e.g. oil) on which the less corrupt countries are highly dependent. But occasionally, the corruption in another country becomes so intolerable that other countries decide to do something about it. A prime example is the USA's 2012 Magnitsky Act, which was designed to punish (through visa-bans and freezing bank accounts) Russian officials deemed to have played a role in the death of auditor Sergei Magnitsky. The relevance to corruption is that Magnitsky had been investigating fraud among Russian tax officials and police officers, and had then been arrested himself for alleged collusion with an investment advisory company that had reported alleged corruption to the Russian authorities and had in turn been accused by those authorities of tax evasion. Magnitsky's death in custody was highly suspicious. Not unexpectedly, the act soured relations between Moscow and Washington; the Russians soon produced a list of Americans who would not be granted visas, and placed a ban on US families adopting Russian children.

Many readers who prefer a broad definition of corruption will be aware of the allegations made against various international sporting bodies, including the leading soccer organization, FIFA. In early 2014, the most widely reported example related to the bidding process for the 2022 World Cup. Such allegations, whether proven or not, undermine the international legitimacy of such bodies, as well as of the states accused of involvement in corrupt practices.

This chapter has concentrated on the negative effects of corruption. But it would be misleading not to acknowledge that some well-regarded analysts have argued that corruption can sometimes be beneficial. Indeed, some maintain that it can be morally justifiable: a classic situation cited to argue this is of the Nazi prison guard who allows Jewish prisoners to escape in return for a bribe. Exploring the ethics of this scenario involves a long and complex discourse, and is beyond the scope of the present exercise. But the more general point about corruption's possible benefits must be addressed.

In the 1960s, several American and British academics—notably Nathaniel Leff (Columbia University), Joseph Nye and Samuel Huntington (both Harvard professors), and Colin Leys (Sussex University)—argued that we should move away from moralizing approaches towards corruption and instead consider it in rational, functional terms (i.e. the functions it performs). This approach is sometimes called revisionism in corruption studies. They argued—each in his own way and to differing degrees—that developing states could sometimes benefit from corruption, since it could 'grease the cogs' or be a 'tonic' rather than being 'sand in the cogs' or 'toxic'. They maintained that if a state was weak and in various ways dysfunctional, corruption could assist in getting necessary things done.

Some still maintain that corruption is not always a collective bad. For example, Bulgarian analyst Ivan Krastev has argued for a more nuanced approach to corruption relating to investment; favouring domestic investors over foreign ones, perhaps in return for bribes, gives locals a chance to get their foot on the capitalist ladder in post-communist states, where there was previously no bourgeois class. Others have suggested that current Chinese leader Xi Jinping's clampdown on corruption in his country is having a negative impact not only on exclusive shops and restaurants in China, but also on Chinese economic growth and thus the world economy, implicitly suggesting that corruption might be a lesser evil.

A third recent example of this viewpoint can be found in a 2007 article by Luigi Manzetti and Carole Wilson, who argued that many citizens will support corrupt politicians if the state is weak and those politicians can deliver what the citizens want. Such an argument can even apply to strong states. Thus a six-country survey conducted by this author 2004–6 on the connections between party financing and corruption suggested that between 14 per cent (Germany) and 35 per cent (France) of voters—with the figure being around 25 per cent in Bulgaria, Italy, Poland, and Russia—would be more likely to vote in a two-person electoral race for a dynamic but corrupt candidate with a reputation for getting things done than for a 'squeaky clean' but ineffectual one.

Such results are interesting and in many ways counter-intuitive, but need to be 'deconstructed'. First, survey respondents may behave differently in a real-life situation—here, an election—than they claim they would in a survey; but determining whether more or fewer would *actually* vote for the corrupt but effective candidate is extremely difficult. Second, respondents were only given an option between two sub-optimal candidates; in the real world, if there were a dynamic but clean candidate, s/he would provide serious competition to the other two. Expressed another way, the respondents who indicated that they would vote for the corrupt candidate were not clearly demonstrating a preference for corrupt officials, merely one for the lesser of two evils. This all said, evidence from India and Italy makes it clear that voters will sometimes elect candidates they know are corrupt.

While there are still revisionists who maintain that corruption can sometimes be beneficial, a subtly alternative approach is that of Robert Klitgaard, who in the late 1980s argued for an 'optimal amount' of corruption. Klitgaard does not condone corruption, but, perhaps reflecting his economist's perspective, argues that the costs of countering corruption should not exceed the economic damage being wrought by that corruption; the point at which corruption is being maximally combated relative to resources is the optimal amount.

Nowadays, there is widespread—though clearly not universal—agreement that even if corruption may in some specific situations be beneficial, this is only ever short term; eventually, the costs of corruption invariably outweigh the benefits. One of the problems with excusing short-term corruption is that a culture of corruption can be established that is extremely difficult to counter further down the track. Rather than excuse corruption altogether, a better approach is to relativize it, along the lines of Heidenheimer's threefold distinction between black, white, and gray corruption (see Chapter 1). This allows for differentiation or nuancing without resorting to outright apologism.

Chapter 3
Can we measure corruption?

In a 1995 article, Moisés Naím referred to a global 'corruption eruption'. But has the scale of corruption really been increasing? Are some countries really more corrupt than others? In order to answer these questions, we need to be able to measure corruption. Unfortunately, this is a particularly difficult task, in part because we cannot agree on what constitutes corruption.

But another significant factor is the difficulty in obtaining information. With most crimes and acts of misconduct, there are victims who can and often do report their experience to the authorities. But citizens who have paid a bribe are unlikely to report the official who demanded or accepted it. One reason is that the citizen has in most cases him- or herself committed a crime in paying the bribe. Another is that the bribe-payer may fear that the permit to build a house or the passport they received in return for the bribe will be revoked or confiscated, so that reporting the corrupt official would be against their interests. Where an official or other responsible person has not engaged in bilateral exchange—for example, if they have been embezzling funds—the 'victim' is often a large and anonymous organization such as the state or a major corporation that will not even be aware of the losses until a proper audit is conducted, which may happen rarely. Sometimes, the 'victim' is even more abstract, such as 'society'. Finally, all of the scenarios just outlined involve a tangible gain to the corrupt person. But if we include social corruption, it should be obvious why measurement—e.g. of the scale of patronage—would be extremely difficult.

Despite these significant problems, if we are to determine whether the levels of corruption in a particular country or agency are increasing or decreasing compared with those of others, and if we are to reduce them and be able to demonstrate that reduction empirically, then we must *attempt* to measure those levels of corruption.

There are four common methods used to measure the scale of corruption—official statistics; perceptual and attitudinal surveys; experiential surveys; and tracking surveys. This chapter examines these, and then briefly considers less common methods.

Official statistics

For many analysts, the starting point for measuring the scale of corruption is official statistics produced by the state. These are principally one of two kinds—legal and economic. Legal statistics typically report on up to five dimensions of corruption:

1. The number of cases reported.
2. The number of cases investigated.
3. The number of prosecutions.
4. The number of convictions.
5. The sentences meted out.

Such data constitute a starting point, but are highly problematic, especially if used to compare countries. Thus, lower figures—relative to population size—on some or all of the first four variables in Country A than in Country B *might* be because there really is less corruption in Country A, or because the reporting and investigating culture is less thorough in Country A. Citizens in Country A might believe there is little point in reporting suspected or known corruption because the authorities are incompetent, indifferent, or themselves corrupt—whereas the citizens in Country B have more trust and confidence in their law enforcement agencies. Another problem is that many countries do not provide comprehensive—or indeed any—figures explicitly on corruption; data are often buried within broader categories such as economic crime or abuse of office, both of which can include phenomena not generally defined as corruption.

Another type of corruption-related statistic sometimes published by government agencies is economic, notably on the average size of a bribe and on corruption's economic impact. But since it is impossible to identify many actual cases of corruption, it follows that such data can only ever be guesstimates; indeed, they are often based on survey data—e.g. asking respondents how much they have paid in bribes in the previous twelve months, and what the average sum was—which are explored over the next few pages, rather than on more solid foundations.

At best, official statistics are a guide to the *minimum* scale of corruption. But since Country A investigates allegations on a more haphazard basis than Country B, knowing the *minimum* amount reveals little, and can be quite misleading. It is all very well to be able to see the tip of the iceberg, but this tells us nothing about the overall size of the iceberg. Given this, most analysts nowadays prefer methods other than official statistics for assessing the scale of corruption.

Perceptual and attitudinal surveys

The most frequently cited source on the scale of corruption across the world is TI's CPI, a perceptual survey. In this type of exercise, what is being measured is people's perceptions of and attitudes towards corruption—whether they believe the authorities are doing enough to contain it, in which agencies it is most prevalent, etc. The CPI has been produced annually since 1995, and has been described by TI as a 'poll of polls' or 'survey of surveys'. TI does not conduct actual surveys itself in producing the CPI; rather, it nowadays collates and standardizes surveys conducted by others—'independent institutions specializing in governance and business climate'—to produce a score and a rank for each country it has assessed. It will not assess a country or territory unless it has access to at least three surveys, which explains why the CPI never includes all the countries in the world; in 2012, it produced scores for 176 of the approximately 200 countries and territories that currently exist.

Until 2012, the CPI was scaled 0 (highly corrupt) to 10 (very clean), and produced scores to one decimal place (two in the earliest CPIs). This changed in 2012, so that the CPI is now scaled 0 (highly corrupt) to 100 (very clean). While space limitations mean the full 2012 table cannot be reproduced here, Table 1 provides the scores of the top twenty and bottom twenty countries.

The amended scaling system in 2012 was intended to symbolize other more significant changes to the CPI. One problem with the index, which TI itself has long acknowledged, is that since the sources change somewhat from year to year, it is not strictly appropriate to compare results over time. Given the lack of alternative data, many analysts have nevertheless drawn such comparisons; but honest ones emphasize the unreliability of such an exercise, and seek to reduce the severity of the problem by comparing such data with other sources.

Since the number of countries assessed in the CPI varies from year to year, comparing *ranks* over time can be particularly misleading. If country X is ranked 40th one year, and 80th five years later, the unwary could be forgiven for assuming that the corruption situation there has dramatically deteriorated; but if the total number of countries assessed is 80 in the first year and 160 five years later, the situation in country X might in fact be more or less the same as it had been, since it remains right in the middle of the

Table 1 Select results from the 2012 Corruption Perceptions Index

Country or territory	Rank	Score	Country or territory	Rank	Score
Denmark	1=	90	Angola	157=	22
Finland	1=	90	Cambodia	157=	22
New Zealand	1=	90	Tajikistan	157=	22
Sweden	4	88	Dem. Rep. of the Congo	160=	21
Singapore	5	87	Laos	160=	21
Switzerland	6	86	Libya	160=	21
Australia	7=	85	Equatorial Guinea	163=	20
Norway	7=	85	Zimbabwe	163=	20
Canada	9=	84	Burundi	165=	19
Netherlands	9=	84	Chad	165=	19
Iceland	11	82	Haiti	165=	19
Luxemburg	12	80	Venezuela	165=	19
Germany	13	79	Iraq	169	18
Hong Kong	14	77	Turkmenistan	170=	17
Barbados	15	76	Uzbekistan	170=	17
Belgium	16	75	Myanmar	172	15
Japan	17=	74	Sudan	173	13
United Kingdom	17=	74	Afghanistan	174=	8
United States	19	73	North Korea	174=	8
Chile	20	72	Somalia	174=	8

Corruption

pack. Hence, for most purposes, citing a country's score is less potentially misleading than citing its rank, certainly if over time comparison is being made. TI has announced that the new CPI methodology means that from 2012, direct comparison between different years will be permissible; however, the point about scores and ranks will continue to pertain until the number of countries analysed is stabilized.

The CPI has been criticized for many other reasons, including that it seeks the perceptions mainly of business people and specialists, not the general public. This is true of many comparative perception surveys, such as the World Bank's BEEPS (Business Environment and Enterprise Performance Survey) and the World Economic Forum's GCR (Global Competitiveness Report). There are numerous surveys of the general public's perceptions of corruption, but most focus on only one country and have their own particular set of questions. Hence, if the primary interest is in comparing countries, such individual country surveys are of limited value.

Experiential surveys

Some maintain that perception surveys do not reflect the 'real' situation. There are two problems with this charge. First, they imply that someone—perhaps the critic—knows what the real situation is. This is nonsense; *nobody* can know the actual extent of corruption in any society, given definitional disagreements and the phenomenon's inherent secrecy. Second, perception is a form of reality anyway. If potential investors in a country decide not to invest there because of high perceived levels of corruption, the perceptions are impacting upon actions, and are thus a form of reality; as is evident from the centuries-old debate between idealist and materialist philosophers, we live in a world of images as well as substance, and there is no single reality.

Nevertheless, it makes sense to attempt to measure corruption levels in as many ways as possible, and critics of perception surveys often advocate the use of experiential surveys instead. In these, respondents are not asked about their perceptions of corruption, but rather their actual experiences of it. A typical question is 'Have you or anyone in your household paid a bribe in the last twelve months?'. When such surveys were first mooted in the 1990s, many specialists were sceptical, assuming that people would never admit to paying bribes. But by now we have abundant evidence to show that, as long as respondents trust surveyors' assurances about confidentiality and anonymity, many will confess to paying bribes.

Partly in response to criticisms of its CPI, TI introduced a new type of survey in 2003 that combines perceptual, attitudinal, and experiential questions in one survey. This is the Global Corruption Barometer (GCB), which has been conducted every 1–2 years since its introduction. This is described on the TI website as a survey of 'people's views and experiences'. Unlike the CPI, the GCB is conducted by TI itself (using survey companies in the countries being researched), and has the distinct advantage over the CPI that it uses a standardized questionnaire. There is also greater consistency in the survey questions than in the CPI, so that there are fewer problems in making over time comparisons. Conversely, the GCB's coverage is less extensive than the CPI's; from surveying a total of just forty-six countries and territories in 2003—and the results for some of these were very incomplete—the GCB has expanded, so that the 2010/11 survey was conducted in 100; this was an impressive number, but still well below the CPI's. Again, reasons of space mean that only a tiny selection of results can be cited here. But Table 2 provides evidence that many citizens *will* report having paid bribes if asked. In compiling the table, it was decided to include only countries from the top and bottom twenty of the CPI that had been assessed for the 2010/11 GCB, since this renders direct comparison of the two sets of findings easier.

Table 2 Select experiential results from the GCB*
(%; rank-ordered alphabetically on 2010–11 score)

Country or Territory	2004	2005	2006	2007	2009	2010/11
Denmark	2	1	2	2	1	0
Norway	3	4	2	–**	2	1
United Kingdom	1	1	2	2	3	1
Australia	–	–	–	–	–	2
Finland	3	3	1	2	2	2
Switzerland	2	1	1	1	1	2
Germany	1	2	2	–	–	2
Netherlands	2	0	2	2	1	2
Iceland	3	1	2	1	2	3
New Zealand	–	–	–	–	–	4
Canada	1	1	3	1	2	4
Hong Kong	1	0	6	3	7	5
United States	0	1	2	2	2	5
Japan	1	0	3	1	1	9
Singapore	1	4	1	–	6	9
Luxemburg	2	6	6	6	4	16
Venezuela	9	6	21	12	28	20
Sudan	–	–	–	–	–	21
Iraq	–	–	–	–	44	56
Afghanistan	–	–	–	–	–	62

(continued)

Table 2 Continued

Country or Territory	2004	2005	2006	2007	2009	2010/11
Dem Rep. of the Congo	–	–	–	–	–	62
Burundi	–	–	–	–	–	74
Cambodia	–	–	–	72	47	84

* Responses to the question 'In the past 12 months have you or anyone living in your household paid a bribe in any form?'

** Dashes indicate the country was not assessed in that year

Some countries' positions in the CPI and GCB vary a fair amount, and there are one or two surprises in the 2010–11 results: Luxemburg and Singapore appear to have higher rates of bribery than would be expected, whereas Venezuela and Sudan apparently have much lower rates than their 2012 CPI scores would suggest. Nevertheless, the underlying pattern is the same using both survey methods: citizens in affluent and stable democracies are far less likely to pay bribes than are citizens in impoverished dictatorships or unstable states.

Before leaving the GCB, three points need to be made. First, as with all the data presented so far, the word 'appears' has often been used here in analysing them. It is likely that citizens are more afraid in some countries than in others to acknowledge having paid a bribe, which can distort our interpretation of the corruption situation across countries; most social survey data, not only those relating to corruption, should be treated with caution.

Second, the GCB experiential question can potentially tell us much about petty corruption, but is of little use in considering grand corruption, since most citizens rarely if ever come into contact with high-level officials, such as politicians. This is a significant limitation of most experiential surveys, given that elite corruption is usually far more damaging than petty corruption.

Finally, analyses of the correlation between the CPI and the GCB findings have been conducted on several occasions since the first GCB was published in 2003; it is reassuring that the level of correlation is relatively high.

In addition to the GCB, a number of other surveys examine the corruption experiences of the general public, of which the International Crime Victim Survey (ICVS) is arguably the best known and regarded. Unfortunately, this is not conducted on a regular basis, and the country coverage varies considerably from one survey to the next. Nevertheless, it is worth noting that the correlation between the CPI and the ICVS has also been examined, and proves to be strong; this is encouraging, since it gives the user greater confidence in the reliability of the various perception surveys. Readers interested in the corruption experiences of the business sector should consult both the BEEPS mentioned previously and the International Crime Business Survey (ICBS), though the latter has unfortunately been conducted only once (2000; it did have smaller predecessors in the 1990s).

Another useful 'one-off' at the time of writing was the 2014 Eurobarometer Special Report on Corruption, though this survey is now supposed to be conducted on a regular basis. For the first time in a Eurobarometer survey, members of the EU public were asked for their actual experiences of bribery; while some 12 per cent (0 per cent in the UK!) claimed to know personally someone who takes bribes, only 4 per cent had themselves been asked or expected to pay a bribe. However, this overall average is potentially misleading, since the figure was significantly higher in some countries than in others. Thus 25 per cent of Romanians and 29 per cent of Lithuanians had been asked or expected to pay a bribe; at the other end of the spectrum, and more or less in line with findings using other methods, the proportion was very low (below 1 per cent) in Scandinavia and Finland, Germany, Luxemburg, Portugal, and the UK.

Tracking surveys

An imaginative approach to measuring corruption was introduced by the World Bank in the 1990s; this was the tracking survey, of which there are two main types—the Public Expenditure Tracking Survey (PETS) and the Quantitative Service Delivery Survey (QSDS). These are somewhat technical for an introductory book, but their basic methodology and rationale can be readily explained.

During the 1990s, the World Bank became increasingly concerned that funds it was allocating to developing countries were in many cases not reaching those for whom they were intended. For instance, most of the funding intended by the Bank to help educate Ugandan primary schoolchildren never got to them. The Bank therefore deployed a method for tracking its funds at each administrative level down to the individual primary school, and worked with the Ugandan government from 1996 to implement this. The results were very impressive; the average of 13 cents in the dollar actually reaching primary schools in the period 1991-5 rose to over 80 cents by 2001. This was an example of a PETS.

A good example of a QSDS survey is provided by Bangladesh. The World Bank suspected that much of the funding it was allocating for the provision of healthcare there was being either wasted or used improperly. A tracking system was devised that mainly involved unannounced visits to healthcare facilities in 2002 to determine who was absent. This revealed that some 35 per cent of healthcare workers of various kinds—and more than 40 per cent of doctors—that were being paid in part from the Bank's funds were not actually at work when they were supposed to be, leading the principal researchers in the project to refer to 'Ghost Doctors'. While some health workers had legitimate reasons for being absent, it emerged that many doctors were moonlighting—running a private practice at times when they should have been working for the publicly-funded salary they were drawing. Again, merely conducting the survey led to an improvement in the situation.

A significant advantage of tracking surveys is that they not only measure corruption, in being able to provide 'before and after' statistics, but simultaneously help to reduce it, which is ultimately the most important reason for trying to measure it. Unfortunately, like all corruption measurement techniques, tracking surveys have drawbacks. For example, they can only measure the level of corruption in a specific situation, whether that be sectoral (education, healthcare, etc.) or regional; they are not suitable for gauging the overall scale of corruption in a country. They are also very expensive, in terms of both time and money: indeed, relative to the scope of their coverage, they constitute the most expensive method analysed here. Finally, they only work well if the authorities in the target countries are willing to cooperate with the surveyors. Thus, while the Ugandan government was highly supportive of the World Bank's approach and objectives, the Tanzanian authorities proved to be much less cooperative over several PETS run by various agencies from 1999 to 2004—perhaps being loath to participate in what they saw as external interference—with the result that the PETS conducted there were less successful.

Other methods

In addition to the four principal methods already analysed, researchers can use several others for gauging the extent of corruption in a given context. One is to organize *focus groups*. These usually comprise 8-12 people, typically members of the general public rather than specialists, who are encouraged to discuss a topic for between 45 minutes and two hours. The researcher acts only as a moderator or facilitator, not a participant. Most research projects involve several such groups, and the discussions are usually taped (sometimes just notes are taken). After the focus groups have convened, researchers analyse the discussions to identify the dominant perceptions and attitudes; computer software such as N-Vivo can assist in this.

An advantage of focus group research is that it is cheaper and easier to organize than conducting a large-scale survey. But unlike a mass survey, the results of which would be statistically significant if the sampling were conducted properly and the number of respondents was at least 1,000, focus group research cannot be treated as reflective of the views of the general public; the sample is too small. Moreover, since group participants could report each other to the authorities following the discussions, this method is unsuitable for measuring experiences of corruption.

Although most focus groups are organized on a face-to-face basis, there have recently been moves towards organizing online focus groups; most analysts consider these less satisfactory than the traditional method, however. But another method that *is* mostly run online, via e-mail, is the *Delphi method*. Here, researchers contact specialists—typically between eight and fifty—rather than members of the general public, invite them to respond to a number of questions, and subsequently to rank-order responses. The researchers then produce a final report, which is sent to each of the respondents; this is their incentive to participate in the project.

Delphi surveys have several advantages: they are inexpensive; they involve people who know more about the specific topic than members of the public do; the participants do not all have to be in one place at one time; and they can simultaneously provide detailed information on corruption and specialist advice on how best to reduce it in specific contexts. On the downside, they can take a long time if specialists are busy; securing a reasonable level of consensus can prove difficult; and the results are not statistically significant.

A third method is to conduct interviews. For instance, a study of police corruption might involve interviewing a small number of people from a selection of appropriate agencies: for a small-scale research project, it might make sense to interview six police officers, six investigative journalists, six judges, six members of anti-corruption NGOs, and, in countries where these have been established and publish their findings, six members of a commission established to investigate corruption (e.g. the Knapp and Mollen Commissions in the USA; the Wood and Fitzgerald Commissions in Australia). The similarities and differences between these groups, and even within them, can then be analysed and interpreted.

For most projects, the optimal approach is to use semi-structured interviews. These comprise a list of standard questions to be asked—so that the researcher can directly compare responses across and within groups—but also allow for free discussion following these questions; after all, interviewees often raise issues that are relevant, but of which the researcher had previously been unaware, and having a closed interview (i.e. adhering strictly to a previously prepared questionnaire) usually means the researcher misses valuable 'insider' information and perspectives.

The fourth method has changed significantly as a research tool in recent years; this is content analysis. In the past, when perhaps a ten-year run of one or more newspapers had to be analysed in a limited time, this approach involved careful selection of articles, possibly specific periods, and rigidly adhering to a set format. With the advent of online sources and search engines, it is now relatively inexpensive, quick and easy to see how, for example, the media in a given country or countries have been reporting corruption—frequency of reports, type and level of corruption reported, etc. Reports on corruption produced by investigative commissions are another type of document that can be systematically analysed, and are often an invaluable source of information; a major problem is that they are rare.

While testing this would require another type of research, it is reasonable to infer that the public's perceptions of corruption are influenced by the amount and type of coverage the media have been giving it. Content analysis of the media would not measure corruption per se, though in many countries in which the authorities do not systematically publish official statistics, newspapers sometimes convey pieces of the statistics jigsaw when reporting, for example, a speech by the Interior Minister. But this method can be used to make intelligent assumptions about how and why citizens or businesspeople have the perceptions of corruption they have.

Fifth, researchers can use case statistical analysis. This involves detailed analysis of a large number of actual cases of corruption (often based on reports in the media, court proceedings, and interviews), following which the results are aggregated and compared to identify patterns. This tends to be more useful for studying corruption in a particular sector or region than for generalizing about whole populations, but can reveal much about the salience of different types of corruption within a given group.

A relatively new method is experiments. An increasing number of social scientists are moving away from other methods and towards experiments to test their hypotheses. One reason is that many believe this method provides more convincing causal explanations than most other techniques: did A really *cause* B, or are they simply related in some way that we cannot satisfactorily explain?. For instance, we might want to know whether the perception that customs officers in Country A are noticeably more corrupt than their equivalents in Country B is based in fact. To test this, we could try to smuggle something relatively minor (so as to reduce the risk of more than a small fine if discovered), such as twice as many duty-free cigarettes as are formally permitted, into both countries, and count how often customs officers offer to turn a blind eye in return for a small bribe.

The experimental approach is attractive, but can be problematic when applied to a sensitive area such as corruption. For instance, testing the corruption proclivity of traffic police officers by seeing how frequently one can avoid a speeding fine by offering a bribe raises tricky ethical issues. If we really are speeding, this statistically increases the likelihood that our experiment would endanger innocent members of the public. And defenders of civil rights would question whether it is justifiable to place traffic police officers in what could be seen as an entrapment situation. While it is difficult to devise an appropriate solution to the former issue, the latter could be addressed by ensuring that the experiment involved only sting operations (i.e. designed to identify only officers who were already believed to be corrupt) rather than entrapment (i.e. where a person who would not normally break the rules is presented with such a tempting opportunity that they take it); readers are reminded here of the distinction between grass-eating and meat-eating. In other words, the researchers would not *offer* a bribe, thus tempting normally honest officers, but would wait to be asked for one.

The two scenarios just described, with the customs and police officers, both involve experiments in real-life situations, and are therefore called field experiments. But another type of research— laboratory-based experiments—simulates scenarios in a controlled environment. Like field experimentation, this form of research into corruption levels and proclivity is recent, dating from the early 2000s. But pioneering work in this field has already suggested, for example, that while females in developed societies are generally less corruptible than males, the picture is less clear-cut in developing societies.

Readers can imagine the many ethical and practical problems that can arise in different kinds of experiments, both field and laboratory-based. It should also be clear that the results of laboratory-based experimentation, for instance to determine whether citizens in some countries are more tolerant of corruption than in other countries, have to be treated with caution. Not only do we often need to think 'outside the box' in interpreting results, but the generalizability of the findings must also be questioned if the number of people examined is small. Then there is the important question about the relationship between controlled experiments in a laboratory and actual everyday behaviour; some participants in experiments might act quite differently in a real-world situation. These are just some of the reasons why this method, while attractive in principle, is not without its own problems. But the fact that corruption-related experiments have been successfully conducted, and have given us new perspectives and new questions to address, shows that this method has opened up exciting new possibilities; we just need to continue refining our techniques.

A final very different method is the *proxy* approach. This method is favoured by, for instance, Global Integrity, which argues that since we cannot satisfactorily measure the scale of corruption itself, it is better to examine what is being done to combat it. In its (until recently) annual *Global Integrity Report*, Global Integrity examines measures adopted by various agencies (government authorities, NGOs, the media, etc.) in individual countries, as well as the implementation and enforcement of these measures, and then gives countries an overall score. This is an interesting alternative approach, although there is a danger of taking official declarations too much at face value. Nevertheless, it is useful to know how seriously political elites appear to be taking corruption, what they are doing to raise integrity levels—and what they are not doing. Moreover, Global Integrity relies more on the assessments of local specialists than do many other data sources. As of early 2014, Global Integrity was in the process of changing its methodology, so that the most recent full report was for 2011, when more than thirty countries were analysed.

The answer to the question in the title of this chapter should by now be clear: we *can* measure corruption, but only imperfectly. Numerous methods for measuring corruption have been outlined in this chapter; all have something to offer, but none is without problems. Some measure perceptions, others experiences. Some are intended to capture the 'big picture'—the overall level of corruption in a country—while others target specific agencies, sectors, or regions. Some involve asking the general public, while others focus on the business community—which is one reason why results from a given country sometimes look quite different across surveys. Few are useful for measuring social corruption. We therefore need to have a clear idea of what *exactly* we are trying to determine when we say we want to measure corruption. This said, in almost all research projects, the more methods we use—deploying a so-called 'mixed methods' or multi-angulated (i.e. approaching the measurement issue from as many angles as possible) approach—the better. Unfortunately, this is currently rendered more difficult than it should be because of different country coverage, different wording of questions, etc.

Nevertheless, it is clear that affluent and stable democracies generally appear to have the least corruption, while impoverished dictatorships and troubled states have the most. While there are exceptions to this general pattern, they may be the exceptions that prove the rule. The Nordic states almost always emerge as having very low levels of corruption, whichever method we choose.

In concluding, three important points need to be noted. First, there is no substitute for an intelligent and carefully evaluated choice of methodology (i.e. the methods to be used) and sensitive interpretation of the results. Sophisticated computer-based statistical techniques can assist us in our attempts to measure corruption, but are not an alternative to clear and defensible conceptualization.

Second, almost all methods identified here are relatively new in corruption studies. Although there were by the 1980s a small number of business analyses that included assessments of corruption levels in particular countries, such as the International Country Risk Guide, these were neither widely available nor as focused explicitly on corruption as the surveys that emerged in the 1990s and 2000s. The first CPI was published in 1995, the first GCB in 2003, the first tracking survey was conducted in 1996, while the first experimental research results were published in 2000. And the latest version of content analysis has only been possible with the advent of web-based sources. Hence, we cannot be certain that there really has been a recent 'corruption eruption'; we *can* be certain, however, that awareness of the issue has dramatically increased.

Finally, critics of attempts to measure corruption often charge that our techniques are not merely imperfect, but potentially counter-productive. Thus, potential donors might opt not to provide aid to a country because its elites are shown by various methods to be creaming off much of it. Fortunately, two of the world's leading agencies for combating corruption—TI and the World Bank—are now very aware that cutting off aid to highly corrupt countries is likely to hurt those who most need it far more than it hurts the corrupt elites. They have therefore been addressing this problem in concrete yet sensitive ways; tracking surveys are just one of many potential solutions.

We are still at an early stage of empirical research into corruption, and it is not surprising that there remain many teething problems. In particular, we are still weak at measuring grand corruption. But our techniques are constantly being refined, to which the welcome changes to the CPI in 2012 testify. At the end of the day, imperfect but constantly improving measurement is better than no measurement at all, which plays into the hands of the corrupt.

Chapter 4
Psycho-social and cultural explanations

Any serious attempt to explain corruption has to be holistic.
People are corrupt for numerous reasons, and even where there is
an identifiable primary motivation, this differs from one person or
group to the next. It would therefore be naïve to assume there is
one underlying general explanation, such as greed or opportunity.
Yet we need to identify the various factors that, in combination,
explain corruption; otherwise, attempts to control corruption
will be futile. In this chapter, the focus is on individuals, their
relationship to society, and how cultures might relate to corruption.
Factors are isolated here purely for the sake of a clearer narrative;
in the real world, they interact, overlap, and combine with each
other in complex ways.

This point about interaction explains the choice of theoretical
framework for the analysis in this and the next chapter. The
approach is based on Anthony Giddens' structuration theory,
which holds that we cannot fully explain human activity in terms
of either individual freedom of choice and actions (agency) or of
everything being determined by the world we inhabit (structure).
Rather, people exercise choice and make decisions partly on the
basis of their own free will, and partly within the context in which
they live. This notion of interactivity underlies the present
analysis, albeit usually implicitly.

Psycho-social factors

Before analysing psycho-social explanations, we need to understand what the term means. The first part refers to the individual: psychology—the study of the mind—focuses on how and why individuals think and behave in the ways they do. Conversely, sociology focuses on the ways societies are structured and operate. So a psycho-social approach combines these two: it examines individuals and their interaction with the social context.

Although psychology focuses on the individual, metaphysical poet John Donne's well-known maxim that 'no man is an island' is very apt when considering what might be seen as purely personal factors. Thus if we start our examination by identifying 'greed' as an explanatory factor, it should be obvious that even this cannot be completely detached from its social context. Wanting 'more' relates to a particular society's norms; many items considered absolute basics in an affluent society, such as a refrigerator or a computer, would be considered luxuries in an impoverished one.

Our second factor also relates to the individual's place in society; this is the need for the respect or recognition of others. In his book *The End of History and the Last Man*, Francis Fukuyama referred to our basic need for *thymos*—an idea he adapted from Hegel—which is an ancient Greek word referring to the human desire for recognition. Similarly, singer Phil Collins refers in 'Both Sides of the Story' to the street kid who carries a gun because, without it, no-one respects him. If corruption (e.g. accepting bribes) means increased spending power and the social cachet that accompanies this, or gives an individual a feeling of power over others (e.g. through exercising patronage), then it can be interpreted partly in terms of *thymos*.

Related to the previous point is that some individuals become corrupt because of their own ambitiousness. If upward mobility channels appear to be blocked, corruption—such as paying a bribe to enter university, which then becomes a 'learned' response to obstacles once one reaches a position of authority—can assist ambitious individuals to circumvent the roadblocks.

In seeking to explain why some people become involved in organized crime, James Finckenauer and Elin Waring coined the term 'sucker mentality', meaning in part that if a person is treated by the dominant value system as an outsider, then he or she would be foolish to live by the system's values. A similar argument can be made about corruption. If a member of a minority ethnic group that was discriminated against by the majority group were to reach a position of authority and not take personal advantage of this, they could be seen as a loser or 'sucker'. A variation on this is that some become corrupt to counter boredom and routine in their lives—tolerance of which would be another dimension of a 'sucker mentality'—and experience the thrill of rule-breaking.

Another theory of criminality that can contribute to a better understanding of corruption is opportunity theory. As its name implies, this approach maintains that people will often take advantage of opportunities that arise—for instance, being 'in the right place at the right time'. This theory can be linked to rational choice theory, which for the purposes of the present discussion can best be understood in terms of cost–benefit analysis. If there is little likelihood of being caught, and a high probability of receiving only a light sentence anyway if discovered and convicted, then the potentially high returns of corruption would lead an (amoral) interest-maximizing individual to engage in it.

In one way or another, all of the factors so far elaborated are positive stimuli to the individual. But there are also negative stimuli. One is a sense of insecurity. This is sometimes purely psychological, a function of an individual's own personality, and might relate to insecurity experienced during childhood. But another relates to the individual's current situation in society. If there is growing unemployment, or the government has just announced its intention to substantially reduce the number of public servants, some officials will seek to take advantage of their office not because of ambition or egotism, but to accumulate funds while they can. This can be called the 'squirrel's nuts' syndrome.

The previous point segues nicely into the next, namely the question of need. In many weak states—for instance, those undergoing transition after a revolution or in a post-conflict situation—officials are not paid in full, or are paid late, or, in extreme cases, are not paid at all. In such circumstances, engaging in corrupt acts is, at least initially, a survival mechanism.

A third negative stimulus is pressure from others, either peers or superiors at work, or perhaps a partner. Regarding the former, research on police corruption demonstrates that officers who join corrupt units are often pressured in various ways into participating in the unit's corrupt activities; if they refuse, they can be ostracized or threatened with reprisals, including violence. But if they then do not blow the whistle on their colleagues' corruption, they are complicit, and in this sense themselves corrupt. However, this form of corruption is ultimately based on fear, not a desire for more power or material wealth.

Fear can also explain why some officers do not report organized crime activity of which they are aware. Crime gangs sometimes threaten to harm the children or partners of police officers if the latter report their activities. In such cases, police officers are still being corrupt, since they are abusing their office for private reasons (i.e. putting family before duty to the state and society). However, in this type of case, if the officer's inaction is discovered and s/he is prosecuted, judges or the officer's superiors should treat them leniently, since this constitutes an example of either white or grey corruption.

Another type of misconduct also relates to fear, but would generally be perceived as either grey or black corruption. This is where a person in a responsible position abuses their office because of blackmail, often based on a form of entrapment. An example of this is of a Chinese Finance Minister who resigned in August 2007, allegedly—the Chinese authorities have been noticeably quiet about the reasons—because of the discovery of an affair he had been having with a woman working for Taiwanese intelligence. This type of entrapment is called 'setting a honeytrap (or honeypot)'.

Another criminological theory that can help us better understand the 'why' of corruption is labelling theory. In its original format, it is particularly associated with Howard Becker; a later theory, John Braithwaite's 'shaming' approach, is closely related to it. This basically contends that once a state or society labels someone a criminal (or shamed them), they are likely to remain one unless steps are taken to redress this. The argument is that it is better not to treat a first-time offender, at least for less serious misconduct, as a criminal if crime rates are not to increase; reintegration is better than alienation. This argument can be modified and applied in the corruption context. For example, if the media continually claim that customs officers are more corrupt than they actually are, then some officers who previously did not engage in corrupt acts may begin to, on the grounds that 'they don't trust us anyway, so to hell with them!'. The perception that one is not trusted can be a strong impetus to rule-breaking.

The focus so far has been on factors that might explain why individuals become corrupt. But a final theory we can borrow from mainstream theories of crime addresses the question of why more people do *not* engage in anti-social activity. After all, if rational choice theory is correct, then surely there should be *more* corruption until disincentives clearly outweigh incentives.

In a 1969 book, Travis Hirschi developed 'control theory', which, in this original version, holds that the strength of ties to one's group constitutes an important explicator of behaviour. Assuming the group is basically law-abiding (in a broad sense), then close bonds between the individual and the group act as a control on the individual. Conversely, weak ties mean that the individual is more likely to pursue his or her own interests, without consideration for the impact of this on others. In a later analysis, Hirschi joined forces with Michael Gottfredson to develop what they boldly claimed was a general theory of crime. This also focuses on control, but this time more on the individual's self-control. But since they argue that the individual's self-control is partly the result of socialization processes, it is clear that their approach fits well with the interactive structuration approach advocated here. It should also be evident that control theory helps to explain why more people in authority do not take improper advantage of their positions.

Before leaving psycho-social explanations, one that is almost certainly relevant but essentially impossible to prove is the concept of innate morality. According to many philosophies and religions, we are all born with an inbuilt sense of right and wrong, and social contexts will determine the extent to which we pursue one or the other.

Cultural explanations

Why is it that countries in North-Western Europe appear to have much lower levels of corruption than those in South-Eastern Europe, or that most European countries appear to have lower levels of corruption than most in Latin America or Africa? Within Latin America, why do Barbados, Chile, and Uruguay appear to have less corruption than other countries in the region, and why is Botswana the star performer—being perceived as the least corrupt—among sub-Saharan African states? Some analysts have sought to explain this in terms of cultural differences. It will be recalled that culture in this context refers to the dominant values, attitudes, and behaviour in a society. These may relate to the impact of religious and philosophical traditions, how much trust there is, whether or not a country has ever been colonized, and whether or not it has recently been a dictatorship.

Starting with religious and philosophical traditions, there are discernible correlations between the levels of perceived corruption as measured by the CPI (see Chapter 3) and dominant religion. Thus Protestant countries tend to be perceived as less corrupt than Catholic countries, which are seen as less corrupt than Orthodox countries—while Christian countries as a whole are apparently less corrupt than most Muslim ones.

There are some interesting and imaginative suggestions as to why Protestant countries tend to be less corrupt than Catholic ones, ranging from historically based theories—Protestantism arose as a reaction to the corruption of the Catholic Church, and this abhorrence of corruption has filtered down the centuries—to the fact that Catholics can offload their sins via the Confessional, whereas Protestants have to accept personal responsibility for theirs. Another explanation proffered by analysts such as Ronald Inglehart is that more hierarchical systems tend to be more corrupt, and Catholicism is more hierarchical than Protestantism.

But correlations can be spurious, and the patterns may well be misleading. For example, the GDP per capita income, the level of democracy, levels of trust, and the overall quality of governance are all at least as strongly correlated with perceived (and experienced petty) corruption levels as the religious or philosophical cultural variable. How is it that four predominantly Sinic countries with similar traditional philosophical cultures—China, Hong Kong, Singapore, and Taiwan—apparently have such different levels of corruption? Since Hong Kong and Singapore are small political units while China is huge, perhaps this helps to explain the differences? Certainly, countries with relatively small populations dominate the 'least corrupt' category of the CPI, suggesting that size of country is somehow connected with the culture of corruption.

Yet there are also small countries in the most corrupt category—forcing us to re-think, or at least refine, this assumption.

One scholar who has tested the hypothesis that religious traditions help to explain, or at least are closely correlated with, differing perceived corruption rates is Daniel Treisman. In an excellent analysis of the causes of corruption, he finds that while Protestantism correlates well with lower levels of corruption, no strong correlation is discernible in the case of other religious traditions.

A second cultural value often mentioned in the literature is attitudes towards the family and the state. According to this argument, in cultures in which loyalty to one's relatives (familism) and friends generally takes precedence over loyalty to the state, certain forms of corruption, particularly social ones, are more prevalent than in less family-oriented cultures. As with so many aspects of social research, how one defines and measures the degree of familism will affect the results of a research project. Certainly, countries in which the extended family is a more salient feature than in more individualistic cultures do generally appear to have higher corruption rates, so that this factor could be part of the explanation for the differences between North-Western and South-Eastern Europe (and of the differences between Protestantism and Catholicism noted earlier). But care must be exercised here, since most measurement techniques focus on economic rather than social corruption. While there might be a correlation between high levels of economic and social corruption, this has to be investigated empirically.

Dominant attitudes towards the family, the state, and authority relate to a state's legitimacy. Where the general public basically trusts the state and accords a regime a high level of legitimacy, there is likely to be less corruption. It should be fairly obvious that this is a chicken-and-egg issue, however; citizens will trust the authorities more if most of their officers are considered honest.

Eric Uslaner has demonstrated that it is not only the level of trust in the authorities that correlates with perceived corruption levels, however; how much we trust others, particularly people we do not know, is also a factor. Basically, low levels of social trust correlate with higher levels of corruption.

Our fifth variable focuses on the impact of the past on present attitudes and behaviour. Some argue that former colonies are more prone to corruption. The argument has several strands. Leigh Gardner maintains that since colonial administrations generally lacked the capacity to collect taxes themselves, they relied on local tax collectors, who often took bribes from members of the local population instead of collecting the appropriate taxes; by the time the colonial power withdrew from the colony, this practice had become well-entrenched, and continued into the post-colonial era. Another perspective on the impact of colonialism is that, since the state authorities were for long seen by the local population as externally imposed and hence illegitimate, both citizens and some local officials had no qualms about cheating the state; again, this attitude often carries over into the post-colonial setting.

While the impact of colonialism may often help to explain corruption levels, there are limits to its persuasiveness. At the very least, the argument needs refining. For example, there is evidence that former British colonies are in general—notable exceptions include Nigeria and Pakistan—less corrupt than former French or Portuguese ones, perhaps indicating that the level of legitimacy during the colonial era varied. Another point is that certain powers often seen as imperialist, such as Russia within the USSR, were themselves perceived to be highly corrupt, so that many in an alleged colony—such as Estonia—eschewed corruption so as not to appear to be 'stooping' to the colonizing power's level.

One legacy many imperial powers left former colonies is the legal system. These are often classified in a simple binary way as common law and civil law systems. The former, based on legal precedent, is typical of Anglophone countries, whereas the latter, based on a written code, is dominant in continental Europe. It has been suggested that there is typically less corruption in countries with a common law system than in those with civil law systems. This is because the judiciary in the former tends to be more independent of the political elite, rendering them less prone to engage in social corruption such as patronage. It is also because the judicial system is less transparent in civil law systems, partly because the role of the general public—which can act as a control on potentially corruptible judges—is reduced, given the rarity of trial by jury.

On the other hand, precisely because it is usually more independent of the political elites, the judiciary in a common law system may find it easier to get away with accepting bribes from the private sector. Yale University's Susan Rose-Ackerman therefore wisely argues that either system can promote corruption; whether this becomes a salient feature of the judiciary or not depends less on institutional arrangements than on the values and attitudes of the judges themselves (the judicial culture—see Figure 4). This in turn usually relates to the general culture of the country they inhabit—the dominant attitudes in society towards corrupt behaviour.

This reference to judicial culture leads to the broader issue of the dominant attitudes in society towards the law—whether or not there is a rule of law culture. By now there is ample evidence that a well-developed rule of law culture correlates closely with low levels of corruption. Conversely, high levels of arbitrariness by the authorities correlate strongly with high levels of corruption.

Arbitrary behaviour by the state is far more typical of authoritarian states than of democratic ones. Just as past experience as a colony may have some influence on attitudes towards, and hence the scale of, corruption in a given society, so too can past experience under an authoritarian or totalitarian system leave a legacy that

4. Judicial corruption is nothing new.

impacts upon contemporary values. For instance, Communist systems encouraged various coping mechanisms, in part because of the shortages of consumer goods. Bribes could ensure access to goods in short supply. But another common practice was *blat*, which was briefly considered in Chapter 1. According to Alena Ledeneva's classic analysis of this, *blat* is:

> the use of personal networks and informal contacts to obtain goods and services in short supply and to find a way around formal procedures. The word is virtually impossible to translate directly into English.

Another reason why citizens in the USSR and other Communist societies developed sophisticated ways of circumventing the system was that it was such a closed one. In line with Lenin's view of Communist parties as comprising the politically most aware (the 'vanguard' of society), they were in theory highly selective in their admissions; yet securing advancement in the system almost always necessitated joining the Party. Hence, many people were prepared to cultivate overly cosy ties to others they believed could help their careers.

Many contemporary states that were never under Communist rule but were or still are authoritarian also share features conducive to the development of a culture of corruption. Most are former colonies, and the impact of the colonial legacy has already been considered. But in addition, the very fact of an authoritarian system, in which elites typically set a bad example by creaming off a country's wealth and stashing it in opaque offshore bank accounts, while denying citizens the right to investigate and openly criticize such practices, reduces the populace's trust in the system and hence that system's legitimacy. Citizens and officials thus feel less compunction about breaking the system's rules and taking advantage of that system when the opportunity arises.

One of the more imaginative examples of empirical research into corruption conducted in recent years endorses the notion that officials from some countries are much more corrupt than their counterparts elsewhere. Raymond Fisman and Edward Miguel examined illegal parking by diplomats in New York City between 1997 and 2005, and concluded that 'There is a strong correlation between illegal parking and existing measures of home country corruption. Even when stationed thousands of miles away, diplomats behave in a manner highly reminiscent of officials in the home country.' This certainly constitutes a cultural interpretation of corruption.

Social construction of corruption

Any comprehensive analysis of the culture of corruption in a given context (country or region) needs to consider how the issue of corruption is framed or constructed. Analysts such as András Sajó maintain that the 'problem' of corruption in many transition (and, implicitly, developing) states is exaggerated by hypocritical Western states because of the latters' own vested interests. While it cannot be denied that there is plenty of corruption in developed states, Sajó is probably going too far by suggesting that citizens in transition countries are not as concerned about corruption as Western critics claim; survey results indicate that he is exaggerating the extent of public indifference to corruption.

But there is another aspect of the social construction of corruption that deserves a mention. Some commentators have justifiably highlighted the fact that corrupt officials tend to be treated much more leniently than 'regular' criminals, and have related this to the types of labels we attach to different crimes. Thus organized crime is generally seen as typical of the 'underworld', whereas white-collar crime in a broad sense, including many forms of corruption, is treated as 'upperworld' crime. In fact, a burglar may take money from—and traumatize—a handful of people, whereas a corrupt official (or executive, if we use the broad definition of corruption) may have a serious negative impact on hundreds, thousands, or in rare cases even millions of people, so that the respective punishments may be quite inappropriate, relative to the impact of the crime. Here, dominant attitudes in society—culture—that treat upperworld crime as somehow less serious than underworld crime can help to explain why penalties for the former are typically less severe than for the latter; lighter punishments mean fewer disincentives for officials to break the rules.

It has been shown that numerous attributes of both individuals and cultures can help us to understand differing rates and types of corruption across countries. But we must be wary not to push these explanations too far; countries with similar religious traditions can have very different levels of corruption, for example, while many young people have traumatizing experiences but do not engage in criminal or other forms of serious anti-social behaviour as adults.

A final point is that we must also be wary about too readily accepting the claims of elites—or even academics—that what outsiders criticize as 'corruption' is simply part of a given country's culture, and that it is inappropriate for others to condemn 'traditional practices'. Malaysian sociologist and author of several books on corruption Syed Hussein Alatas, for example, criticized Westerners who argued that corruption in developing countries was more tolerable than in developed countries because it was simply part of their culture. For Alatas, such a stance was condescending, and he called for universal condemnation of corruption.

Chapter 5
System-related explanations

Explanations of corruption that focus just on the individual are incomplete; we are all subject to and conditioned by the context in which we live and work. Since culture has already been considered, structural or system-related factors are the focus of this chapter; for the sake of analytical clarity, these are separated into economic and political.

Economic factors

In recent years, several aspects of economic systems and policies have been identified as correlating with corruption levels. One of the most popular focuses on the extent to which the state is involved in the economy. This argument has been advanced by, among others, Vito Tanzi of the IMF. Expressed crudely, the claim is that the more a government is involved in the economy, the more corruption there will be. Intuitively, such an argument seems plausible; after all, greater state involvement in the economy usually means a larger bureaucracy, as well as higher levels of interaction between state officials and businesspeople, both of which are conducive to corruption. More state interference often means more opportunities for officials to 'rent-seek'—here meaning that they can secure additional, improper income by selling decisions favourable to an individual or firm prepared to pay for them.

Yet research by John Gerring and Strom Thacker reveals that there is no clear correlation between, on the one hand, the size of the state apparatus or how much the state interferes in the economy in terms of business licensing and demanding compliance by businesses and, on the other hand, corruption levels. The World Economic Forum produces an annual report on the global competitiveness of economies (Global Competitiveness Report; GCR), based partly on how many permits and other forms of state-initiated paperwork are required to start and run a business. The rankings of the top and bottom ten countries in the 2012 CPI can be compared with their rankings in the 2012/13 GCR's 'Burden of government index' to demonstrate this (the question was 'How burdensome is it for businesses in your country to comply with governmental administrative requirements [e.g. permits, regulations, reporting—the lower the rank, the less burdensome]?').

Table 3 demonstrates that the level of corruption is not strongly correlated with the amount of government interference in the economy, with apparently highly corrupt countries such as Tajikistan and Cambodia being less bureaucratic than Denmark, Norway, and Canada—while the former two, plus Chad, Kyrgyzstan, and Libya, were all assessed as less bureaucratic in 2012 than Australia, which has very high compliance requirements.

However, the GCR's overall Global Competitiveness Index (GCI), which includes far more variables than the 'Burden of government regulation', suggests a closer correlation. While New Zealand and to a lesser extent Australia are outliers in Table 4, the variation between the perceived level of corruption and the overall level of economic competitiveness is much less than the variation in Table 3.

Another economic variable to consider is *privatization*. Privatization of an economy that has been largely state-owned creates considerable opportunities for corruption, as some businesspeople offer bribes or kickbacks to gain unfair advantage

Table 3 Perceived corruption levels compared with the level of government regulation

Country	CPI Rank 2012	GCR Burden of Gov't Regulation Rank 2012/13	Country	CPI Rank 2012	GCR Burden of Gov't Regulation Rank 2012/13
Denmark	1=	69	Kyrgyzstan	(135)	92
Finland	1=	6	Yemen	(136)	119
New Zealand	1=	14	Cambodia	(137=)	42
Sweden	4	31	Tajikistan	(137=)	22
Singapore	5	1	Libya	(139)	61
Switzerland	6	16	Zimbabwe	(140)	107
Australia	7=	96	Burundi	(141=)	121
Norway	7=	64	Chad	(141=)	95
Canada	9=	60	Haiti	(141=)	115
Netherlands	9=	34	Venezuela	(141=)	143

Note: The number of countries analysed in the GCR and the CPI differs (144 and 176 respectively for 2012). To render the two rankings comparable, those countries in the CPI not included in the GCR have been removed, and the remaining countries re-ranked out of 144. In short, the bottom ten CPI countries in Table 3 are the lowest-ranked that also appear in the GCR, which explains why the 'bottom ten' CPI states in Table 3 are not the same as the bottom ten in Table 1; brackets are used in Table 3 to highlight this.

over others in the tendering process. This was a major explanatory factor of high corruption levels in post-communist transition states in the 1990s. But privatization has also been a key feature of the neo-liberal (or Washington Consensus) approach to economic management that has swept the globe since the late-1970s, and there have been allegations of major corruption scandals relating to privatization even in countries such as Germany (albeit in that case relating to privatization of post-communist eastern Germany).

Table 4 Perceived corruption levels compared with the overall level of economic competitiveness

Country	CPI Rank 2012	GCI Rank 2012/13	Country	CPI Rank 2012*	GCI Rank 2012/13
Denmark	1=	12	Kyrgyzstan	(135)	127
Finland	1=	3	Yemen	(136)	140
New Zealand	1=	23	Cambodia	(137=)	85
Sweden	4	4	Tajikistan	(137=)	100
Singapore	5	2	Libya	(139)	113
Switzerland	6	1	Zimbabwe	(140)	132
Australia	7=	20	Burundi	(141=)	144
Norway	7=	15	Chad	(141=)	139
Canada	9=	14	Haiti	(141=)	142
Netherlands	9=	5	Venezuela	(141=)	126

* See note to Table 3 for explanation of the use of parentheses here.

However, there can be a silver lining to the corruption problem that so often arises as states sell off assets to the private sector. This is that the privatization process usually has an end-point, or at least becomes less salient a feature of economic policy, as a government decides it has privatized most or all of the enterprises it considers appropriate. On the other hand, another key feature of neo-liberal approaches to economic management is that governments should *outsource* tasks and services for which they had previously assumed direct responsibility. Typically, outsourcing involves calls for tenders from private companies, and hence creates new opportunities for corruption. Moreover, unlike the situation with privatization, outsourcing creates ongoing opportunities for corruption. For instance, a city might decide to outsource the public transport system; but to ensure that the private companies running the system do not become complacent, the city insists on a new tendering process every five years—creating opportunities for corruption each time the contract is renegotiated. The connection between corruption, privatization, and outsourcing has been seen as a major factor explaining increased corruption in the UK during the 1990s; David Hall argued that 'Public sector contracts and concessions are the single greatest source of corruption in the UK which has been fuelled by government privatization initiatives.'

Advocates of neo-liberalism emphasize what they claim is the superiority of free markets over mixed economies (those in which there is a division of labour and ownership between the state and the private sector), and in doing so contribute in various ways to corruption. For instance, neo-liberalism's encouragement of privatization and outsourcing results in the dismissal of many state officials, however loyal, hard-working, and long-serving they may be. This focus on 'downsizing', a term now largely replaced by the less negative sounding 'right-sizing', often results in a heightened sense of insecurity and a marked decline in loyalty to their employer among officials, both of which are highly conducive to increases in corruption; they can result in the 'squirrel's nuts' syndrome mentioned in Chapter 4. One other aspect of neo-liberalism that can encourage corruption is the focus on ends rather than means; achieving ambitious targets often takes precedence over due process.

Neo-liberalism's focus on maximizing the freedom of the market is closely related to the economic approach of globalization, which also seeks to minimize the role of states in the economy and to maximize the freedom of markets, especially in the area of international trade. Writers such as Japan's Kenichi Ohmae have referred in this context to a 'borderless world'. But this term can be misleading: although globalization has reduced the barriers to international trade and made the movement of *capital* around the world ever freer, it has not clearly made the movement of *people* easier. While there are examples of the movement of people becoming freer—notably Europe's Schengen zone, in which people can travel from country to country without needing to show a passport—in other ways it has become more difficult for people to cross borders, especially if they want to settle in a new country. Thus, despite greater freedom of movement *within* the Schengen zone, it has become more difficult to enter it, leading some observers to refer to 'Fortress Europe'. This development encourages corruption, as desperate citizens of impoverished or conflict-ridden countries seek a better life by paying people-smugglers, who in turn bribe customs and border officials to turn a blind eye as their 'cargoes' cross state frontiers.

An oft-cited formula in corruption analyses is Robert Klitgaard's equation, $C = M + D - A$, where C stands for corruption, M for monopoly, D for discretion, and A for accountability. According to this approach, the more discretionary powers officials have, the more corruption there will be—unless those officials are highly accountable. One area in which this often pertains is taxation. If there is a progressive tax system (i.e. higher tax rates for higher incomes or profits), then some individuals and businesses will offer bribes to tax officials to confirm that income or profits were less than they actually were. A study by the Policy Group in India in the mid-1980s estimated that more than 75 per cent of government tax auditors took bribes, while some 68 per cent of taxpayers using Certified Tax Accountants to lodge their tax returns had paid bribes.

Unfortunately, the assumption that a flat-rate system significantly reduces such opportunities must be questioned. While such a system means that tax officers cannot corruptly agree to confirm lower income or profit to keep an individual or company out of a higher tax bracket, they can still be bribed to confirm lower taxable income than was actually made, thus assisting tax evasion.

An economic variable correlating highly with corruption
levels is the overall wealth of a country, as measured by the
GDP per capita. Numerous sophisticated economic analyses
demonstrate this correlation; for our purposes, the most
important finding is that, with few exceptions, the poorer a country,
the higher the level of corruption. A simple way of demonstrating
this is to compare the GDP per capita of the top and bottom
twelve countries of the CPI (see Table 5—this time reverting to
the full listing of the CPI, so that the bottom twelve are as
in Table 1).

**Table 5 Perceived corruption levels compared with GDP
per capita**

Country	CPI Rank 2012	2011 GDP per capita (US\$)*	Country	CPI Rank 2012	2011 GDP per capita (US\$)*
Denmark	1=	59898	Burundi	165=	247
Finland	1=	48678	Chad	165=	1006
New Zealand	1=	36919	Haiti	165=	732
Sweden	4	56755	Venezuela	165=	10728
Singapore	5	51242	Iraq	169	6019
Switzerland	6	83087	Turkmenistan	170=	5725
Australia	7=	62081	Uzbekistan	170=	1545
Norway	7=	99173	Myanmar	172	*no data*
Canada	9=	50578	Sudan	173	1538
Netherlands	9=	49886	Afghanistan	174=	614
Iceland	11	44031	North Korea	174=	*no data*
Luxemburg	12	111913	Somalia	174=	*no data*

* World Bank figures

While the correlations in Table 5 are weaker than some considered in this chapter, Table 5 nevertheless demonstrates clearly that higher levels of corruption are related to lower standards of living as measured by GDP per capita. Thus, while the lowest per capita income in the top ten (least corrupt) countries was in New Zealand, its figure was still almost three and a half times higher than the best performer in the CPI's bottom ten (Venezuela), which itself was much higher than that of the next two wealthiest countries in the bottom ten, Iraq and Turkmenistan.

In Figure 5, the close correlation between perceived corruption levels (2012) and GDP (2011) is clear; each of the 22 points represents one of the following: what are perceived to be the eight least and eight most corrupt states, and the six states right in the middle of the CPI rankings (position 88).

But what if a high average GDP per capita is very unevenly distributed? Does this affect the GDP/corruption correlation? A useful analysis is that by You Jong-sung and Sanjeev Khagram published in 2005; in a sophisticated study of 129 countries, they

Corruption

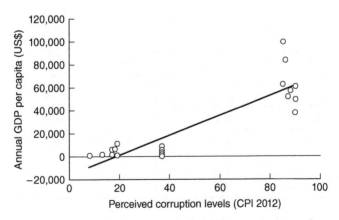

5. **Perceived corruption levels compared with GDP per capita graph.**

demonstrate that higher income inequality usually means a higher level of corruption.

Let us now consider the relationship between corruption and international economic factors. It is often posited that countries that adopt protectionist measures in foreign trade—prioritizing domestic suppliers over foreign ones, for instance through imposing import levies—are more corrupt than more open economies. Pushan Dutt has tested this empirically, and concludes that countries with protectionist systems do have higher levels of corruption among state bureaucrats than countries that encourage more liberal trade. His research is rigorous and persuasive. But we should not overlook the fact that the scale of corruption can refer also to the average size of bribes, not simply to how many officials accept bribes. Thus, more liberal trade policies mean that foreign companies that are much larger and wealthier than domestic companies in a developing or transition country can offer much bigger bribes than can the locals. Some bribes offered by corporations to secure overseas contracts are considerable. In 2010 Swiss freight forwarder Panalpina admitted in a US court to having paid US$49 million in bribes in seven countries in the period 2002–7. One of the companies it had assisted in this way was the oil giant Royal Dutch Shell, which confessed to having paid US$2 million to Nigerian subcontractors to circumvent 'export formalities'.

Transition and developing states often seek and secure financial aid and loans from wealthier states, and from international organizations such as the IMF and the World Bank. Unfortunately, and all too often, much of the aid and loans finishes up in the offshore bank accounts of those states' elites. In short, what is intended to be a benefit for an impoverished population often proves to be yet another—very profitable—source of corrupt opportunities for elites. According to Transparency International's *Global Corruption Report 2004*, among those countries that have suffered the biggest losses because their leaders were creaming off these and other funds are Indonesia

(Suharto), the Philippines (Marcos), Zaire (Mobuto), Nigeria (Abacha), and Haiti (Duvalier).

Political factors

The claim often made that the larger the state apparatus, the more corruption there will be, has been questioned by some, who cite Sweden as a good example of a country with a large state apparatus and apparently low levels of corruption. But this might be merely an exception to the rule. A more persuasive argument has been made in a 2012 article by Go Kotera, Keisuke Okada, and Sovannroeun Samreth. Based on an analysis of eighty-two countries, they conclude that the relationship between corruption and government size is complex, and a third variable has to be included, namely the level of democracy. It seems that an increase in the size of government often results in reduced corruption in a robust democracy, but will increase corruption levels in a country with little or no democracy.

It was demonstrated in Chapter 3 that, according to our imperfect measurement techniques, stable established democracies appear to be less corrupt than dictatorships or unstable systems. It is certainly the case that, while many citizens in the latter types of system have had direct experience of paying bribes—first and foremost to police officers, healthcare workers and educationists—most Westerners encounter such petty corruption much less often. If we return to our list of countries perceived to be most and least corrupt, and compare these ranks with the type of political system (as assessed in the *Economist Democracy Index* (EDI) *2012/13*), this pattern emerges clearly (Table 6).

Among the countries perceived to be least corrupt, Singapore is the only real outlier; otherwise, the pattern is clear—all of the most corrupt states that appear in both the CPI and the EDI are either hybrid (semi-authoritarian) or authoritarian, with the bottom six all being authoritarian.

However, Table 6 may be a little misleading. Thus, there has been no shortage of *high-level* (elite) corruption cases in the established democracies in recent years. A key feature of many of the West's high-profile cases of corruption since the 1990s is that they relate to the funding of political parties. Individual leaders and other politicians in mature democracies appear more likely to engage in corrupt practices designed to help their party than to fill their personal coffers (although, of course, helping their party to win an election can ultimately benefit them personally); this point pertains to both the Helmut Kohl and Jacques Chirac cases, for instance. While such party-related corruption also sometimes applies in developing and transitional states, there are far more alleged and proven cases in these than in developed states of elite corruption for personal enrichment.

Even here, however, the distinctions drawn are often too stark. As noted in Chapter 2, one of the most difficult aspects of corruption analysis is deciding whether or not to include political lobbying. Both sides of this debate have merit, and we shall here sidestep this difficult issue in cases where lobbying is transparent. But much lobbying is opaque, and can overlap with 'state capture'. According to Joel Hellman and Daniel Kaufmann, this was hampering the political and economic reform processes in many post-communist transition states. Their argument has been challenged, for example by analysts who maintain that it is too tidy—that rather than unethical businesspeople buying off legislators and public (civil) servants, they often become part of the political elite themselves. In a sense, both positions are correct and incorrect; the situation varies, and what is true of one country is not true of another. What is clear, however, is that the phenomenon is by no means confined to transition or developing states.

Thus legislators sometimes sell their votes in parliaments in developed states too. In the UK, there have been numerous

Table 6 Perceived corruption levels compared with levels of democracy

Country	CPI Rank 2012	EDI Rank 2012/13	EDI Classi-fication 2012/13	Country	CPI Rank 2012	EDI Rank 2012/13	EDI Classi-fication 2012/13
Denmark	1=	4	FD	Burundi	(157=)	125	A
Finland	1=	9	FD	Chad	(157=)	165	A
New Zealand	1=	5	FD	Haiti	(157=)	116	H
Sweden	4	2	FD	Venezuela	(157=)	96	H
Singapore	5	82	H	Iraq	(161)	113	H
Switzerland	6	7	FD	Turkmenistan	(162=)	162	A
Australia	7=	6	FD	Uzbekistan	(162=)	161	A
Norway	7=	1	FD	Myanmar	(164)	155	A
Canada	9=	8	FD	Sudan	(165)	154	A
Netherlands	9=	10	FD	Afghanistan	(166=)	152	A
Iceland	11	3	FD	North Korea	(166=)	167	A

Key: The EDI classifies countries as Full Democracies (FD), Flawed Democracies (none in Table 6), Hybrid systems (H), or Authoritarian (A).

Note: The bottom eleven countries are those listed in both the CPI and the EDI; since the latter assessed fewer states and territories (167) in 2012 than the former (176), the allegedly most corrupt countries in Table 6 are not identical to those in the actual CPI, a fact highlighted by the use of parentheses.

'cash-for-questions' scandals, in which members of both houses of parliament have been accused of raising issues in parliament and improperly promoting the interests of lobbyists—some of them actually investigative journalists posing as lobbyists—in return for bribes. In 2013, such allegations were made against a former Labour Minister (Lord Cunningham) and a former Conservative front-bencher, Patrick Mercer. In the Cunningham case, a House of Lords enquiry determined there was insufficient evidence of misconduct to pursue it. But Mercer resigned as Tory whip, and then announced his imminent resignation from parliament in April 2014, just before the publication in May of a Standards Committee report finding him guilty of deliberately evading the rules of political advocacy and recommending a six-month suspension from the House of Commons.

For German social theorist Max Weber, a well-functioning modern state should not merely be a democracy, but also have a well-developed rule-of-law culture; indeed, Weber was more concerned with the latter than with the former. The Washington DC and Seattle-based World Justice Project has been producing a *Rule of Law Index* (RLI) since 2010; a total of 97 countries was assessed in the 2012–13 RLI. Unfortunately, the RLI does not include an aggregate single ranking for countries. But Factor 5 ('Open Government') comprises four variables that most rule-of-law specialists would see as key components of it: that laws are publicized and accessible; laws are stable; citizens have the right to petition government and participation; and official information is available on request. While this does not cover all key aspects of the rule of law—such as that no-one is above the law, and laws should not be retroactive—it is nevertheless a useful aggregation of several factors that should be examined in determining how closely a country adheres to the rule of law. Given this, we can once again consider perceived corruption levels, this time as they appear to relate to the rule of law (see Table 7).

Yet again, and despite exceptions such as Singapore, Kenya, Kyrgyzstan, and Ukraine, there is a marked similarity between most countries' perceived level of corruption and the extent to which the rule of law is observed in them. Indeed, the amount of corruption in a country can be seen as one indicator of the extent to which there is a rule-of-law culture.

In 1999, following complaints from several developing states that it was being unfair in focusing in its CPI on the bribe-takers (the demand side of corruption) and essentially ignoring those offering

Table 7 Perceived corruption levels compared with the rule of law

Country/ Territory	CPI Rank 2012	WJP's RLI Rank 2012	Country/ Territory	CPI Rank 2012	WJP's RLI Rank 2012
Denmark	1=	8	Kenya	(86=)	64
Finland	1=	7	Nepal	(86=)	79
New Zealand	1=	4	Nigeria	(86=)	90
Sweden	4	1	Pakistan	(86=)	92
Singapore	5	19	Bangladesh	(90=)	89
Australia	(6=)	5	Cameroon	(90=)	95
Norway	(6=)	3	Ukraine	(90=)	62
Canada	(8=)	6	Kyrgyzstan	(93)	61
Netherlands	(8=)	2	Cambodia	(94)	83
Germany	(10)	16	Zimbabwe	(95)	97
Hong Kong	(11)	10	Venezuela	(96)	84
Belgium	(12)	21	Uzbekistan	(97)	88

Note: As with most tables in this chapter, countries have been re-ranked from their original CPI ranking because of the smaller number of countries included in the RLI; this is again highlighted by the use of parentheses.

or agreeing to pay bribes (the supply side), TI introduced the Bribe Payers' Index (BPI). This asked businesspeople—in the early years of the BPI only in developing states—to name the countries whose companies were most likely to offer bribes to secure contracts. The BPI is published every 3-4 years, and nowadays also asks businesspeople in developed and transition states to assess the propensity of firms from various countries to pay bribes. Since the index focuses on the world's major exporters, it ranks less than thirty countries. The results of the 2011 BPI can be seen in Table 8 (scaled 0-10—higher numbers indicate a lower propensity to pay bribes).

Table 8 The Bribe Payers' Index 2011

Country	Rank	Score
Netherlands	1=	8.8
Switzerland	1=	8.8
Belgium	3	8.7
Germany	4=	8.6
Japan	4=	8.6
Australia	6=	8.5
Canada	6=	8.5
Singapore	8=	8.3
United Kingdom	8=	8.3
United States	10	8.1
France	11=	8.0
Spain	11=	8.0
South Korea	13	7.9
Brazil	14	7.7
Hong Kong	15=	7.6
Italy	15=	7.6
Malaysia	15=	7.6
South Africa	15=	7.6
Taiwan	19=	7.5
India	19=	7.5
Turkey	19=	7.5
Saudi Arabia	22	7.4
Argentina	23=	7.3

(continued)

Table 8 Continued

Country	Rank	Score
United Arab Emirates	23=	7.3
Indonesia	25	7.1
Mexico	26	7.0
China	27	6.5
Russia	28	6.1

A point to note from Table 8 is that while the rankings correlate closely with the CPI rankings, the range (6.1–8.8) is much smaller than the latter's for those countries included in the BPI.

The fact that Western countries' firms appear to be less likely to pay bribes should not blind us to the fact that a number of major Western-based transnational corporations have in recent years been found to have been paying bribes or kickbacks to secure contracts overseas or other forms of favourable treatment (e.g. lower taxes); in addition to those already cited, other notable examples include Halliburton, Hewlett-Packard, and Pfizer.

But such corporate misconduct sometimes generates another type of corruption that is more typical of developed than of transitional or developing states, namely where senior government officials are aware that companies based in their country are paying bribes overseas, but turn a blind eye or even attempt to cover up such malfeasance. A prime example is the major political scandal about UK arms sales to Saudi Arabia. This relates to the Al-Yamamah arms deal, in which British arms manufacturer BAE and its predecessor were accused of paying huge bribes to secure sales to the Saudis. This is a long and convoluted case. Suffice it to say that the deal was Britain's largest ever trade deal; that British Prime Minister Tony Blair was accused of a cover-up after he blocked an investigation of the allegations in 2006 on the grounds of national security; and that BAE agreed to pay a fine of US$400 million to the US authorities in 2010 under a plea bargain that meant it was not found guilty of bribery (it pleaded guilty to false accounting and making misleading statements). Despite this fine—one of the largest in US legal history—and a smaller but still substantial one paid to the UK's Serious Fraud Office at about the same time, the fact that BAE was not found guilty of actual bribery meant it was not debarred (blacklisted) by the World Bank and other international agencies, and thus remained free to tender for future arms deals.

A significant political factor that often helps to explain corruption is a country's historical legacy, which was considered in Chapter 4. Reactions to the legacy can also impact upon corruption levels. Thus, many post-revolutionary states seek to replace a large number of laws across a range of areas—property, elections and party financing, welfare, taxation, etc.—in difficult conditions, often resulting in delays ('legislative lag'). Typically, corruption thrives in a situation where old laws have been discarded, and replacement laws have either not yet been adopted or else are brand new and contain numerous loopholes.

A different legacy is often found in post-conflict states. Such countries were in many cases subjected to international sanctions or even full embargoes during the conflict period; in this situation, some governments encouraged both corruption, and collusion between state officials and organized crime, in order to obtain supplies. Behavioural patterns established in such situations have often continued after the conflict has ended. A prime example is Serbia. Trade sanctions were imposed in 1991 and not lifted until 1996. In the latter year, the Serbian Prosecutor-General acknowledged that his country would have been unable to function were it not for smuggling; while this was carried out primarily by crime gangs, it also involved collusion by the authorities.

Some states are so dysfunctional or ineffectual that they have been labelled 'failed states'. This term is unfortunate, since it can be interpreted to mean that such systems are beyond redemption. Adjectives such as 'troubled', 'disrupted', and 'fragile' have therefore been proposed as alternatives. These are preferable terms, since they connote serious problems in these systems without implying that they are beyond hope. Nevertheless, it must be acknowledged that there is a close correlation between the level of functionality of a state and its perceived level of corruption. This can be readily seen in Table 9, which compares countries' ranks in the CPI and FSI (Failed States Index in 2012—fortunately renamed the Fragile States Index in 2014).

A final political variable is the gender balance in government. In a short but influential 2001 article, David Dollar, Raymond Fisman, and Roberta Gatti argued that political systems with a high proportion of women in politics generally have lower levels of corruption than those with less female representation. But this argument has been challenged by Hung-En Sung, who maintains that it is not the percentage of women, but rather the robustness of democracy, that determines corruption levels.

Most correlations identified in this chapter have been with *perceived* levels of corruption, as reflected in the 2012 CPI. But a leading analyst of the causes of corruption, Daniel Treisman, has argued that while the sorts of correlations made here—and others, such as dependence on fuel exports—are interesting and explain up to 90 per cent of cross-national variation, they are also problematic, since 'measures of actual corruption experiences, based on surveys that ask business people and citizens in different countries whether they have been expected to pay bribes recently, correlate with hardly any of these factors once one controls for income'. Treisman therefore suggests the use of more experience-based surveys. But the reader is reminded that these tend to pick up only low-level corruption, whereas elite-level

Table 9 Perceived corruption levels compared with state's fragility

Country	CPI Rank 2012	FSI Rank 2012*	Country	CPI Rank 2012	FSI Rank 2012*
Denmark	1=	3	Burundi	165=	160
Finland	1=	1	Chad	165=	174
New Zealand	1=	7	Haiti	165=	171
Sweden	4	2	Venezuela	165=	95
Singapore	5	21	Iraq	169	169
Switzerland	6	4	Turkmenistan	170=	96
Australia	7=	13	Uzbekistan	170=	138
Norway	7=	5	Myanmar	172	157
Canada	9=	9	Sudan	173	175
Netherlands	9=	11	Afghanistan	174=	172
Iceland	11	12	North Korea	174=	156
Luxemburg	12	6	Somalia	174=	177

* The scaling in the CPI and the FSI goes in opposite directions—i.e. the lower the number in the CPI, the better, while the opposite is true in the FSI; the FSI scaling has therefore been reversed here for comparison with the CPI—the higher the FSI rank, the more fragile the state appears to be.

corruption typically has a more serious impact—and is more likely to be picked up by perceptions surveys.

Moreover, correlations do not prove causality, and there comes a point at which intuition and personal observation enter the equation. Although our techniques for determining the primary causes of corruption are now highly sophisticated and constantly being refined, we must always be alert to the potential dangers of both inappropriate generalizations from too few cases (inductive reasoning), and of seeking to explain individual cases on the basis

of broad generalizations (deductive reasoning). There is clearly
still a long way to go in researching and explaining corruption.

To conclude: the analyses cited in this chapter are—appropriately,
given its title—concerned with systemic or structural explanations.
But the reader is reminded of the need for a holistic approach to
corruption, based on structuration theory. Neither systems nor
agents are fully autonomous or determining: they are interactive.

Chapter 6
What can states do?

Corruption is what social scientists call a 'wicked' problem, meaning that it is so complex that it can only ever be partly solved; it can be controlled, but never completely eradicated. The state has a key role to play in managing this wicked problem, using 'stick' (disincentive), 'carrot' (incentive), 'administrative and technical', and 'other' methods.

Stick measures

The most obvious 'stick' states can use to reduce corruption is the legal system. One reason sometimes cited by the Botswanan authorities for apparently being the least corrupt country in Africa is that they have a prosecution rate well above the international average. Prosecutions can be of both bribe-takers and bribe-givers.

But prosecutions are not the only consideration; conviction rates and the severity of the penalties also matter. If penalties for those convicted of corruption are lenient, the justice system will be ineffective as a deterrent. Some countries do mete out harsh sentences for corruption. In early-2011, a Pennsylvania-based judge was sentenced to 28 years' imprisonment for wrongly sentencing thousands of children to junior prisons in return for substantial bribes from two businessmen who built and managed private juvenile detention centres; this was known in the US as the 'kids for cash' scandal.

Unfortunately, stiff penalties are the exception globally; the sentences passed on those convicted of corruption are typically soft. In March 2014, a San Diego (USA) court sentenced a border inspector to just 7½ years' imprisonment after finding him guilty of corruptly colluding with drug and people smugglers for almost a decade. But even this was relatively severe in comparison with most other cases. If we use the broad definition of corruption that includes misconduct in the private sector, the short prison sentence (two years and nine months) and short probation period (12 months) given to two executives found guilty in 2008 of serious involvement in the Volkswagen 'sex, bribes and corruption scandal' that emerged in Germany in 2005 were criticized for being too lenient.

Sometimes, those convicted of corruption receive lenient punishments because they have cooperated with the authorities in identifying others engaged in the impropriety. An example is of a political consultant sentenced in Texas in January 2014 to only 10 months' imprisonment (plus a fine and post-prison probation) for corruption; it was made clear that this was a lighter sentence than he would otherwise have received because he 'spilled the beans' on corruption between construction companies and local officials, and on a former judge, resulting in several convictions.

But those proven to have acted corruptly often do not face criminal proceedings at all, merely administrative ones. While the effect of penalties such as dismissal from one's post can be embarrassing, they rarely have as serious a negative long-term impact as a prison sentence, and are thus less of a deterrent.

On the other hand, ten states include the death penalty as a possible punishment for corruption, although China is the only one to use this regularly. Several state functionaries have been executed or threatened with this in China in recent years. While death penalties there are commonly suspended for corrupt senior officials, who finish up serving long prison sentences, those who *have* been executed include the former deputy mayors of Hangzhou, Shenyang, and Suzhou. The death penalty was rarely used in Vietnam until 2013; but public concern there about corruption saw at least three bankers sentenced to death in 2013 and 2014 for embezzling state-run banks.

Draconian penalties are not the only problems involved in using the legal system to fight corruption; abuse of that system is also an issue. In many countries, the judicial system is highly politicized and the rule of law weakly developed. Under such conditions, defendants are often assumed to be guilty unless proven innocent, and people who do not appear to objective observers to be corrupt can be framed and convicted for purely political reasons (e.g. being a member of a political party that has been challenging the authoritarian ruling party, or having criticized a country's leader).

Another problem can arise in states at the other end of the political spectrum. Sweden is so committed to the defence of individual civil liberties that it forbids its law enforcement agencies from mounting either sting operations (against suspected criminals) or entrapment operations (against people not already suspected of criminal activity). While there are strong rule-of-law arguments supporting Sweden's position on entrapment, the arguments against sting operations are much weaker, and mean that a potentially powerful anti-corruption tool is not being used. Moreover, Sweden is inconsistent in this area, since it allows mobile phone intercepts on possible clients of prostitutes (while prostitution is legal in Sweden, using a prostitute's services is illegal).

If officials lead expensive lifestyles that appear incommensurate with their declared incomes, the state should investigate this. In many countries, officials are now required to declare their income and assets, as a way of reducing corruption. But many corrupt officials simply understate these. This is why in-depth auditing of their incomes and expenditure, including access to bank accounts, is in principle an appropriate measure for the state to adopt.

Unfortunately, there are limits to the efficacy of such an approach. An obvious one is that some corrupt officials, especially at the elite level, will deposit their ill-gotten gains in opaque offshore accounts to which their government authorities have no access. Another problem is that some civil rights activists argue that such investigations are an invasion of privacy and therefore unacceptable in a rule-of-law based democracy. But when the potential harm of corruption is borne in mind, this argument is weakened; victims of corruption also have rights, and if income can be shown to have been legitimately acquired, those investigated should have nothing to fear. Of course, there is the danger that some states will act in an arbitrary manner; but this is more likely in authoritarian states in which the individual has few rights anyway, so that the civil rights argument is largely irrelevant in such cases.

While courts are meant to administer justice, legislatures are responsible for passing laws. But all too often laws relating to corruption are either non-existent or else seriously flawed. Sometimes, the laws are ambiguous or deficient, rendering it easier for defence lawyers to make cases for clients accused of corruption that the law does not clearly prohibit or apply to a particular type of misconduct. States therefore have a responsibility for tightening up anti-corruption legislation. Although the explanation for weak or ambiguous laws sometimes relates to the newness of a system—it takes time to devise and then refine laws—another factor is that parliamentarians often have a vested interest in not passing tough, unambiguous legislation; their own shady dealings could be brought to light and punished.

Many states now have dedicated anti-corruption agencies (ACAs). Singaporean authorities often attribute their success in combating corruption partly to the establishment of the world's first independent ACA, the Corrupt Practices Investigation Bureau (CPIB). This was established in 1952, and has a strong record in keeping corruption levels in Singapore at low levels. Another example of a very effective ACA is Hong Kong's Independent Commission Against Corruption (ICAC, established 1974), while the Botswanan Directorate on Corruption and Economic Crime (DCEC), established in 1994, also enjoys an enviable record. But while these three agencies are often taken as model ACAs, others are far less effective.

ACAs perform poorly for numerous reasons, including inadequate funding and blurred lines of responsibility. The latter is often the result of successive governments establishing new bodies without disbanding existing ones, so that there is an unclear division of labour, resulting in buck-passing between agencies. A leading expert on Asian corruption, Jon S. T. Quah, argues persuasively that a major reason for the success of the CPIB in Singapore and the ICAC in Hong Kong is that both have sole responsibility for combating corruption (a point that also applies to Botswana); in most other countries there are multiple agencies. A fourth problem is that such agencies are often less independent of the bodies they are to investigate than they should be. A number of ACAs around the world tasked with looking into police corruption are required to use the police themselves to conduct the investigations. In contrast to such practices, the CPIB and the ICAC have their own investigative powers, and answer directly to the Singaporean Prime Minister's Office and Hong Kong Chief Executive respectively.

In some countries, a popular way of using the 'stick' against those found guilty of corruption is public shaming. For example, the South African Justice Minister announced in February 2013 that the government would be publishing the names of those convicted of corruption, once it had decided which media to use for this; in

June, the names of forty-two people convicted of particularly serious cases of fraud and corruption were published on the South African government website.

Closely related to the practice of naming and shaming corrupt individuals is the policy of publicly blacklisting (debarring) private companies found to have engaged in the corruption of public officials. Singapore has been a trailblazer in this area too. In January 1996, the Singaporean authorities debarred five major corporations, including Siemens (Germany), BICC (UK), and Pirelli (Italy), from tendering for Singaporean contracts for five years after they were found to have bribed a Singaporean official. Siemens has also been debarred in several other countries—Italy, Slovakia, and Brazil—and accused of corruption in yet others (e.g. Argentina).

Another approach that can be used in attempts to penalize corporations for offering bribes is to litigate. The Filipino government did so against Westinghouse after the latter constructed the Bataan nuclear power plant in the 1980s that never became operational before it was decided in 1999 to mothball it; it had not been commissioned because it was located too close to a major earthquake fault line and to a volcano that erupted in 1991. Unfortunately, the Filipino authorities were unable to persuade the US to try Westinghouse for bribe-giving under the latter's Foreign Corrupt Practices Act, for reasons that remain unclear. Nevertheless, the possibility of litigation remains.

A final stick method is when authorities threaten some future penalty for those considering engaging in corruption; a powerful one is the threat of nullifying retirement pensions.

Carrot measures

In the 1st century AD, the Roman historian Tacitus wrote that 'The more corrupt the state, the more numerous its laws.' While a sweeping generalization, there is some truth to this observation, and it is worth considering ways in which states can fight corruption other than by introducing ever more regulations.

Governments can use a range of incentives in their endeavours to reduce corruption. One is to improve the officials' working conditions, particularly their salaries; the success of anti-corruption policies for law enforcement officers in Singapore, Georgia, and to a lesser extent Russia, has been linked by commentators to substantial pay-rises. As with most anti-corruption measures, however, this one is not without problems. Many of the apparently most corrupt states are also among the poorest, and could not afford to raise officers' salaries to the levels at which some commentators believe corruption will begin to reduce. Second, simply raising salaries without simultaneously increasing 'stick' measures often means in practice that corrupt officials opt to accept the higher salaries *and* continue taking bribes; they are in a win-win 'double-dip' situation, whereas the state is in a lose-lose one, since it is paying more to its officers but not increasing state revenue.

States that cannot afford to introduce across-the-board salary increases for groups of officials can adopt an alternative method that is still based on material incentive but is less costly. This is to provide financial rewards to officials playing a positive role in combating corruption. Unfortunately, this approach can backfire. For example, the Hungarian authorities decided several years ago to pay bonuses to customs officers who reported travellers offering them bribes to turn a blind eye to smuggled goods. One officer was so successful that he earned more than the prime minister. This raised suspicions, and it was determined following investigations that the officer had been making false accusations so as to maximize his income. A variant on this incentive approach is to reward officials who are incorrupt or who report corrupt colleagues.

So far, the incentive focus has been on officials. But states can also encourage citizens to report corruption. A common method is to establish anonymous hotlines. Another possibility is to introduce schemes to protect witnesses and whistleblowers (people who report the known or suspected corruption of others). Unfortunately, not only are protection schemes relatively expensive, but the fate of those who blow the whistle or testify against a suspect in court can be worse than that of the miscreants. Whistleblowers from within an organization often find themselves being cold-shouldered by colleagues, and many are eventually either dismissed or themselves choose to leave their job because of mistreatment by colleagues.

Witnesses under protection schemes can fare at least as badly. While such schemes mostly relate to witnesses to violent crimes committed by gangs, it should not be forgotten that police corruption can also involve threatened and actual violence. For their own safety, such witnesses are often given new identities and transferred to new locations. Unfortunately, this can have disastrous effects on their own lives, since they are often moved away from family and friends to a strange environment in which they have to live a lie (i.e. they cannot reveal their true identities). In short, this form of incentive might help with law enforcement, but can have serious negative effects on those who assist the authorities.

Administrative and technical measures

An increasingly popular administrative method for countering corruption is rotation, whereby officials are moved on a regular basis from one office to another. The rationale is that corrupt networks take time to develop, so that frequent changes of personnel are likely to hinder this. While an experiment conducted in Germany suggests this might be the outcome, evidence from India is less encouraging, since it reveals that managers sometimes tell each other who is corruptible and who not. Moreover, frequent moves between offices can mean that valuable aspects of corporate memory and officials' experience is lost. Rotation also has a potential downside for bribe-givers, who may find they have to pay twice for a service—once to the original corrupt official and then again to his or her replacement.

Better auditing can also play a role in countering corruption. In 2003–4, economist Benjamin Olken conducted an experiment in over 600 Indonesian villages introducing road-building projects. At the start of the experiment, only some 4 per cent of such projects were audited by the Indonesian authorities. But Olken announced in each of the villages that *all* projects would now be audited. Using a sophisticated methodology, he calculated that 'missing expenditures' were lower following this initiative by an average of more than 8 per cent, which he saw as a 'corruption tax'. His conclusion was that top-down auditing was an effective anti-corruption method; he further maintained that this approach was more effective than a grass-roots monitoring system.

A somewhat technical approach to anti-corruption is norm setting. Suppose that the government of Mali wants to build a new airport in the capital, Bamako, and calls for tenders. Since the government has been involved in other major infrastructure projects in the past and knows the cost of materials and labour in Mali, it can calculate the approximate costs of a kilometre of runway, and thus produce a norm—maximum and minimum figures for the cost, depending on what a tendering company is offering (e.g. faster completion might cost more than slower). The government should then be suspicious of bids either well above or well below this norm. In the former case, the tenderers might have either factored in corruption 'on-costs' (thus raising the price); in the latter, they might be intending to bribe procurement officials to accept low bids, on the grounds that, having secured the contract, they will subsequently be able to claim cost blow-outs.

An issue with norm setting is that it is unclear whether or not the norms should be revealed to potential bidders. For instance, foreign companies might be at a disadvantage over local companies if the norms are kept confidential, since, unless they have previously worked in the region, they could find it difficult to assess costs accurately. Conversely, revealing the norms could disadvantage local companies relative to foreign ones, since large overseas firms might be able to employ economies of scale and fewer workers if they possess expensive machinery that local firms in developing or transition states do not.

In terms of the sums involved, one of the most serious areas of potential corruption is procurement. Defence contracts can be worth millions—even billions—of dollars, and there have been numerous examples of manufacturers of military aircraft paying substantial bribes to officials to secure contracts. One way to counter this is to introduce open on-line tendering, thus rendering the whole procurement process far more transparent. Unfortunately, many governments, let alone private manufacturers of defence equipment, prefer opacity about defence expenditure, allegedly in the interests of national security.

On-line tendering is just one of numerous anti-corruption methods that involve greater use of technology. Another is the use of CCTV (closed circuit television) at strategic locations, such as at border crossings if there is known or suspected to be a high level of corruption among customs officers. And wider use of automated speed cameras can reduce opportunities for traffic police to accept or demand bribes from motorists.

Since corruption can be found in most agencies in most countries, and since the majority of anti-corruption measures incur costs—which governments usually want to reduce—it is better for states to target corruption seen to be the most damaging rather than all corruption; the assessment of this varies from country to country. In most developed states, for instance, corruption is not a major problem in the traffic police, whereas it often is in serious crime squads, where police officers come into direct contact with criminals who may offer them substantial bribes. States therefore need to produce their own tailored risk (or vulnerability) assessments for a targeted approach.

Other measures

Many observers maintain that the most useful method for combating corruption in the long term is to increase levels of trust in society, and to change public attitudes and morality through ethical education. A problem with this is that it takes a long time, sometimes generations, for it to be effective. Moreover, many factors will counter it while it is being applied, so that it might only ever have marginal impact.

However, limited empirical evidence suggests that dedicated seminars (for officials, executives, schoolchildren, etc.) and certain types of campaign can have an effect on attitudes towards corruption even in the short term. Focusing on the latter, there are two main kinds of campaign, one of which is usually much more successful than the other. The more effective one is where governments raise public awareness of what corruption is, that it is unacceptable, and what role citizens can play in combating it. Conversely, campaigns in which governments declare their intention to clamp down on corrupt officials are typically either limited in their effectiveness or counter-productive. All too often, this second type results in the 'crying wolf' syndrome: citizens are so familiar with 'new' campaigns that, like so many previous ones, are supposed to target high-level corruption but then deliver very little, that they will not believe politicians who claim their campaign is different from earlier ones. Public cynicism and mistrust will be rife.

Sometimes, the problem of corruption in a given country is so serious that radical approaches are required. One, adopted by

Mikheil Saakashvili when he was president of Georgia, is to dismiss all the officers from a given branch of the state, shut that branch down, and then replace it with a new one with new personnel and a new image. Saakashvili did this with the traffic police from 2004 on, and scored major successes.

In some branches of the state, staffs are by tradition predominantly male; police forces are an obvious example. An innovative way of addressing corruption in such branches is to change the gender balance. The traffic police in Peru were in the 1990s criticized by their own government and the World Bank for their high levels of corruption. The World Bank suggested experimenting with a change in the gender balance, since women were considered to be less easily corrupted than men. From 1998, the traffic police in Peru were increasingly feminized. A decade later, Peruvian police spokespersons claimed this policy had been a major success, and that corruption levels among the traffic police had substantially declined. A similar policy, also designed to reduce corruption among traffic police, was introduced in Mexico City shortly after the Peruvians had led the way; again, initial results were encouraging.

However, recent research into the Peruvian situation by Sabrina Karim suggests that, while feminizing the force has seen a decline in corruption, the results are less impressive and clear-cut than officially presented. The correlation between the percentage of women in a given branch of the state and corruption levels is not as strong as sometimes suggested. While the empirical evidence on this is still thin, it has been argued that it is less gender that explains declines in corruption when a force is feminized than newness. Corrupt networks take time to develop, as trust between potentially corrupt officers needs to be established and nurtured. The suggestion is that women can also become highly corrupt when working closely together over long periods.

But there is an interesting twist to this. It appears from limited evidence that women generally trust each other more than they trust men, and vice versa. Partly based on this assumption, Polish police forces have in recent years and where possible been deploying two-person patrols comprising one male and one female officer.

A final gender-related point is that Marilyn Corsianos' research into corruption among US police officers suggests that female officers are much less likely to form corrupt networks than are male officers; if this applies elsewhere, it could help to explain why corruption levels are apparently lower where there is a higher percentage of female officers.

Radical gender re-balancing is not the only innovative method tried by Latin American leaders determined to reduce corruption. Another was adopted in the mid-1990s in the Colombian capital of Bogotá by its then mayor, Antanas Mockus. Like many Latin American cities, Bogotá had a serious problem of corruption among its traffic police. Mockus' highly original approach to this was not merely to disband the traffic police, as Saakashvili did a decade later in Georgia, but to introduce mimes as a way of addressing the city's traffic problems. Instead of being issued with fines—or not, in return for a bribe—those breaking the traffic rules were mocked by a large team of mime artists. This not only improved Bogotá's traffic situation, but also reduced corruption.

A fourth radical approach is based on the maxim 'if you can't beat 'em, join 'em'. During the 1990s, there was a problem of corruption in the Romanian military, whereby officers enrolling conscripts would often sign 'unfit for military service' statements in return for bribes. Rather than attempt to address this problem through greater control, the government adopted a lateral approach, making it legal for those who did not want to engage in military service to buy themselves out. This meant that most of the money—there will always be some who will risk paying a bribe rather than pay the (higher) state fee—that had been going into officers' pockets now went to the state.

A final radical approach is to grant an amnesty to those accused or suspected of corruption. A government can declare it will not examine cases that have already occurred, but will clamp down heavily from the beginning of the following year. This method should only be considered in extreme cases, when corruption is so widespread that it would be unrealistic to expect a new administration to be any less corrupt than the one it is replacing. Such an approach has the distinct drawback that many members of the general public will initially be incensed that corrupt officials are being pardoned, which in turn undermines the state's legitimacy. But if positive results become obvious fairly quickly, then many citizens will see this approach as the lesser of two evils.

So far, the focus has been on the domestic measures that can be adopted by national governments. But states can also cooperate with and learn from external agencies, including other states. Our final cluster of 'other' approaches relates to what states can and should do beyond their own borders.

Until the 1990s, the USA was the only country to have legislation that applied to misconduct by its corporate sector overseas. In 1977, following the Lockheed bribery scandals—whereby a leading US manufacturer of military aircraft was found to have been paying bribes over many years and in several countries to secure overseas contracts—and the general mood against misconduct following the Watergate scandal, the USA introduced the Foreign Corrupt Practices Act (FCPA). This made it illegal for American companies to offer or pay bribes overseas to secure contracts. While this was in practice rarely applied until the late-1990s, it set a precedent, and was used by the US to encourage the OECD to adopt an anti-bribery convention considered in Chapter 7. Recent corporations affected by the FCPA include the world's largest employer, Wal-Mart, which in April 2012 was publicly accused by the *New York Times* of bribery in Mexico; in February 2014, Wal-Mart announced that it expected to pay more than US$200 million over the following twelve months investigating possible breaches of the FCPA.

In recent years, many Western states have adopted similar legislation to the FCPA, though most analysts agree that the new UK anti-bribery act of April 2010 (effective July 2011) has set a new, much higher benchmark. This act, described by some as the world's toughest anti-bribery law, is very wide-ranging, covering bribery at home and abroad by both domestic companies and foreign companies involved with British ones. Moreover, whereas the FCPA does not prohibit facilitation payments (or 'speed money', designed to accelerate bureaucratic processes once a contract has been awarded), the British Bribery Act renders these illegal.

States can help each other to reduce corruption by permitting extradition. Unfortunately, many countries do not permit extradition of their own citizens to other countries, even if the latter can provide evidence of wrongdoing. This plays into the hands of corrupt officials and executives.

Another possibility is for states to introduce laws that forbid their banks from accepting questionable overseas deposits, or at least require banks to notify the authorities about suspicious deposits. The pressure on states to pass such laws intensified in the 2000s in the aftermath of 9/11, as it became clear that terrorists were often able to launder money through banking havens. Despite these pressures, a number of countries continue to permit banking practices deemed by the Financial Action Task Force (FATF—see Chapter 7) to be conducive to money-laundering. As of February 2014, the list was headed by Iran and North Korea—while countries that have in the past been seen as banking and tax havens, such as the Cayman Islands and Nauru, have now been removed from the FATF blacklist. At least in terms of banking, there are ever fewer places for corrupt officials to launder their money.

However, many states could do much more to monitor the banking sector, as demonstrated by the Financial Secrecy Index (FSI) that has been produced since 2009. While this does not indicate corruption levels within countries assessed, it does provide a way of seeing how complicit countries are in corruption.

An obvious point to emerge from Table 10 is that almost all of the most secretive jurisdictions have very small populations. One point that does not emerge from it is that the two countries assessed as having the most transparent banking practices among the eighty-two jurisdictions evaluated in 2013 are Denmark and Sweden, with respective scores of 33 and 32; the UK's score is 40. While the Scandinavian scores are unsurprising, it is noteworthy in light of other assessments we have considered that two other countries with relatively transparent banking systems are Spain and Italy (36 and 39 respectively).

It could be argued that Table 10 is misleading, since it ranks jurisdictions in terms of their financial transparency. But the Tax Justice Network that produces the FSI prefers to rank countries primarily in terms of the *value* of the financial secrecy; this is not calculated simply in money terms, but on the basis of a complicated mathematical formula that need not detain us. But using this method, the top (worst) ten countries look very different (Table 11); several major developed countries clearly need to address the issue of tax and banking havens.

In Chapter 1, the problem of distinguishing a gift from a bribe was considered, and the point made that cultures vary considerably in how they interpret these. This is an area in which states need to better understand each others' viewpoints and traditions. Fortunately, there is a growing trend for states to distinguish gifts and bribes quantitatively, if not qualitatively. More and more governments now acknowledge that it can be offensive for their officials to reject genuine gifts offered by officials from other states and cultures, so that a compromise position is emerging. This is to

Table 10 The most secretive jurisdictions in terms of financial regulations, international cooperation, and anti-money laundering compliance (based on FSI 2013; scaling out of 100)

Rank	Jurisdiction	Secrecy Score
1	Samoa	88
2	Vanuatu	87
3	Seychelles	85
4 =	St Lucia	84
4 =	Brunei Darussalam	84
6	Liberia	83
7	Marshall Islands	82
8	Barbados	81
9 =	Antigua & Barbuda	80
9 =	Bahamas	80
9 =	Belize	80
9 =	Bermuda	80
9 =	Malaysia	80
9 =	Mauritius	80
9 =	San Marino	80
9 =	St Kitts and Nevis	80

specify the maximum value of a gift, usually between US$100 and US$150. Of course, there is always the danger that someone will be offered $150 today and every day for many months, so that the gift does equate to a bribe; legislation allowing gifts therefore needs to incorporate wording that forbids circumvention of the gift/bribe distinction.

Table 11 The FSI 2013—Ten worst offenders

Rank	Jurisdiction
1	Switzerland
2	Luxemburg
3	Hong Kong
4	Cayman Islands
5	Singapore
6	USA
7	Lebanon
8	Germany
9	Jersey
10	Japan

A final way in which states can indirectly assist each other in combating corruption is by setting a good example. If developed states criticize transition and developing ones for corruption, they must do everything possible to keep their own houses in order; the pot calling the kettle black will not contribute to a global reduction in corruption.

A key factor in fighting corruption is political will. Unfortunately, this all too often appears to be absent. But a growing number of states are now showing the requisite political will, for instance in that they will punish corrupt officials, however highly-ranked they are or have been. Between 2012 and 2014 alone, former prime ministers in Cameroon, Croatia, Egypt, Israel, Slovenia, Romania, and elsewhere received prison sentences for corruption.

However, some governments are still sending out mixed messages. While China under Xi Jinping has been making serious efforts to reduce the country's corruption, four Chinese anti-corruption activists were sentenced to between two and three and a half years' imprisonment in April 2014 for publicly advocating that state officials be required to declare their assets. Governments that assume they are the only agents with a role to play in combating corruption are seriously misguided.

In 1990, Harvard political scientist Joseph Nye coined the term 'soft power' to refer to the advisability of improving international relations through more dialogue and less coercion or force (which is hard power). In the 2000s, he argued that the US should pursue a policy of 'smart power' in its relations with other countries, meaning a combination of hard and soft power. In combating corruption, what is needed is 'smart anti-corruption', meaning a combination of stick, carrot, and other approaches. However, the mix will vary from country to country, according to the culture, the type of political and economic system, and the resources available; applying a one-size-fits-all approach will not only not work, but can actually be counter-productive by alienating countries that feel they are being unfairly coerced. Nevertheless, the range of anti-corruption methods included in this far from exhaustive analysis demonstrates clearly that much can be done, given sufficient political will and capacity.

Chapter 7
What else can be done?

The state is only one of many actors with a role to play in controlling corruption. In this final chapter, we consider what can be done by international organizations (IOs), the business sector, and civil society, before evaluating the overall effort at combating corruption.

International organizations

As noted, it is only in the past twenty or so years that the international community has focused its attention on corruption. One reason is that the West, which has been the principal anti-corruption driver since the 1990s, had little interest in pushing an international anti-corruption agenda during the Cold War. The USA, in particular, did not wish to upset its allies by criticizing them for corruption; nor did it want to criticize developing states, which could encourage them to join the Soviet camp. But once the Cold War was over, the gloves were off. In the early-1990s, the US began to complain more loudly that its corporate sector was losing overseas business to companies based in other developed states, none of which had anything to compare with the FCPA (see Chapter 6). In short, the Americans wanted a more level playing field in international business.

It was in this context that what many see as the first major attempt by an IO, the OECD's (Organization for Economic Cooperation and Development's) 'Recommendations on Bribery in International Business Transactions', were issued in 1994. But as its name indicates, this was only a set of suggestions; after all, the Americans had not used the FCPA much anyway.

But by the late-1990s, partly because of the growing influence of TI and the fact that the World Bank began seriously targeting corruption following the appointment of James Wolfensohn as its head in 1995, the international community became increasingly aware that corruption was a serious problem. The OECD's recommendations were given more bite, in the form of an anti-bribery Convention that was adopted in 1997 and came into effect in 1999. This Convention established 'legally binding standards': states ratifying it were required to adopt or modify domestic legislation to conform with it.

A tangible effect of the OECD Convention was that several developed states—including Australia, Germany, and the Netherlands—had to cease granting their corporations tax write-offs for business-related bribes paid overseas. The Convention, to which all thirty-four OECD member states plus seven others (Argentina, Brazil, Bulgaria, Colombia, Latvia, Russia, and South Africa) are now party, has been strengthened several times since 1999, notably in 2009 and 2011. It is described by the OECD itself as the 'the first and only international anti-corruption instrument focused on the "supply side" of the bribery transaction'—meaning that it focuses on the misdeeds of the corporate sector in offering or paying bribes, rather than on the officials who accept or demand them.

Closely linked to the OECD is the Financial Action Task Force (FATF). This was established in 1989 on the initiative of the G7 group of leading economic nations, and was tasked with combating money-laundering. Initially, its focus was primarily on organized crime. But its interest soon spread to terrorism and then to corruption; 9/11 was a major stimulus to this. Its anti-corruption efforts have intensified since 2010, when it began working closely with the G20's Anti-Corruption Working Group on how best to combat money-laundering related to corruption. It has published a number of reports on this since 2011.

Although the OECD Convention applies to only approximately one-fifth of the world's states and territories, these are spread around the globe. In addition, a number of regional anti-corruption conventions have been adopted since the mid-1990s. The first was the Inter-American Convention against Corruption, adopted by the thirty-five member-states of the OAS (Organization of American States) in 1996. More recently, in 2003, the fifty-three member-states of the African Union adopted its Convention on Preventing and Combating Corruption (effective 2006).

The EU (European Union) is generally seen to have begun focusing on corruption in 1995, and produced a convention against corruption among its own officials and those of its member states in 1997. This was followed by a 'Comprehensive Policy Against Corruption' in 2003. In addition, it has engaged in targeted conditionality. For instance, when the EU published its general roadmap for enlargement (*Agenda 2000*) in 1997, it also produced individual analyses of the conditions each post-communist applicant state had to meet to be granted membership. The only issue specified in the 'political criteria' section of each of the ten individual analyses was the need to intensify the fight against corruption.

Another European agency, the larger (forty-seven member-states—all European states except Belarus and Vatican City State) Council of Europe (CoE), adopted a number of conventions and other documents in the late 1990s and early 2000s designed to counter corruption. The first was the 'Twenty Guiding Principles for the Fight Against Corruption' in 1997, which was followed by both Criminal and Civil Law Conventions on Corruption in 1999; the former was strengthened in 2003 (effective 2005). The CoE has also produced recommendations on codes of conduct for public officials (2000) and on political financing (2003).

While the CoE has limited capacity for ensuring compliance by its member-states, the agency it established in 1999—GRECO (Group of States Against Corruption)—to monitor compliance by states with its anti-corruption instruments has enjoyed some success. In 2012, GRECO began analysing the gender dimension of corruption, including its differential impact on men and women, which has attracted increasing attention among those fighting corruption.

Finally, the CoE, sometimes with the EU, has introduced several anti-corruption programmes targeted at particular countries and regions. These include the 'Octopus' projects of the late 1990s, the RUCOLA (2006–7) and PRECOP (2013–15) programmes in Russia, and SNAC-South in Morocco and Tunisia (2012–14); some of these reveal that the CoE occasionally operates beyond Europe.

Of all the anti-corruption conventions, the one endorsed by the highest number of states is UNCAC. This was opened for signature in late 2003, and came into force in December 2005, thus being a relatively recent document; by April 2014, UNCAC had 140 signatories and 171 states parties. It is described by the UN itself as the world's first legally binding anti-corruption document (as noted, the OECD Convention has only forty-one signatories), and is seen by some as the 'gold standard' of anti-corruption documents, despite containing no actual definition of corruption.

International law enforcement agencies also have a role to play in combating corruption. The principal one, Interpol, has its own group of specialists—the Interpol Group of Experts on Corruption or IGEC—that was established shortly after Interpol held its first conference on anti-corruption in 1998. IGEC has produced a set of 'global standards' specifically aimed at reducing corruption in police forces. Interpol sees one of its primary anti-corruption roles as asset recovery, i.e. returning stolen assets to victim countries. In recent years, it has been targeting sports-related corruption, such as match-fixing.

So far, the focus has been mainly on preventative and punitive approaches. But IOs can also play an encouraging role. For example, the CoE praised the Netherlands in 2013 for its approach to combating corruption among parliamentarians and judges.

While most IOs have in recent years introduced policies and measures designed to reduce corruption, the World Trade Organization (WTO) has been criticized for doing too little in this area. Established in 1995, it began in 1996 to consider ways of reducing corruption in public procurement; but external observers have in the past claimed the WTO has made little headway. Notably, then head of TI Peter Eigen published an article in 2003 explicitly criticizing the WTO's lack of progress in combating corruption in procurement. The WTO's Revised Agreement on Government Procurement that became effective in 2014 made reference to corruption, but this was fleeting and essentially tokenistic.

The International Chamber of Commerce has also encouraged the WTO to take a stronger stand by urging it to include corruption as one of the prohibited non-tariff barriers, though this has not happened. Scholar Padideh Ala'I has argued that the WTO's emphasis on the need for greater transparency in international trade has contributed to the fight against corruption, while Philip M. Nichols has rightly noted that the WTO is in principle in a stronger position than most IOs to fight corruption in international trade. While true, this means little if the potential is not exploited;

the WTO's 'member-driven' consensual approach has rendered it a
toothless tiger on many important issues, including corruption.

Banks and TNCs

In the early 20th century, Max Weber argued that the best check
on the state bureaucracy, which would include controlling
corruption, was to have a powerful business class separate from
the state. Unfortunately, the business sector and the government
in many countries are all too cosily intertwined, which bodes ill
for the control of corruption. But both banks and the corporate
sector can in principle play a significant role in combating
corruption.

While many see two IFIs (International Financial Institutions),
the IMF (International Monetary Fund) and the World Bank, as
fulfilling essentially similar functions, this is not so. In the field of
anti-corruption, the World Bank has been much more active than
the IMF. While the latter encourages transparency as part of its
emphasis on good governance, its main practical focus relating to
corruption is on countering money-laundering. But the World
Bank has been working in a number of ways since the mid-1990s
to reduce corruption. Its innovative methodologies for identifying
and measuring corruption were considered in Chapter 3; since
1999, the World Bank has also been debarring (i.e. blacklisting)
companies and individuals that have engaged in various kinds of
misconduct in international trade, including sanctions-busting
and corruption. Since 2011, the Bank has increased the potential
effect of such debarment by cross-listing with the Asian
Development Bank, the European Bank for Reconstruction and
Development, and the Inter-American Development Bank.

One of the most controversial approaches adopted by both the
World Bank and the IMF is to cancel or suspend loans because
of corruption. Both suspended loans to Kenya in 1997 for this
reason. More recently, the World Bank cancelled a $US1.2 billion

loan to Bangladesh in 2012 for what would have been the country's longest bridge because of suspected corruption of Bangladeshi officials by a Canadian engineering firm.

Like other international organizations, the World Bank sometimes praises as well as criticizes. For example, it congratulated Romania in 2002 for its work in reducing corruption in the judiciary (though the EU subsequently criticized Romania for doing too little to combat corruption among its judges).

Responding to criticism, a number of private banks have taken steps to counter money-laundering, which can impact upon high-level corruption in particular. In 2000, eleven leading banks joined forces to create the Wolfsberg Group that produced a set of AML principles. The group has continued to produce principles and guidelines, many on aspects of banking—such as correspondent banking and beneficial ownership—that are important in the fight against money-laundering, but somewhat technical for an introduction like this.

It has been noted that many people now include the corporate sector as potentially corrupt (as distinct from being corruptors). Whether one adopts this broad definition of corruption or the narrow one that focuses on state officials, there is no question that the private sector is a major player in global corruption. While Western media have had a field day since the beginning of the millennium detailing the misconduct of companies such as AWB (headquartered in Australia), SNC-Lavalin (based in Canada), and numerous others, less commonly considered are the actions the private sector can and does take to combat corruption. In fact, there are many possibilities.

A small number of companies have in recent years either threatened to withdraw or have actually withdrawn from countries because of the latters' corruption situations. IKEA in Russia is an example of the former, while Unilever withdrew from Bulgaria in 1997 (for some three years) because of the corruption there.

Many private firms have in recent years adopted Codes of Ethics in their endeavours at least symbolically—and in some cases because of genuine concern—to demonstrate their commitment to raising awareness among their workforces of the need for integrity in business relations. These typically emphasize that bribery is completely unacceptable. In the case of Siemens, one of the TNCs shown to have been particularly unethical in the past, senior management has introduced a major compliance programme since 2008, and is now seen as a model of how a company can seek to redeem itself.

Since at least the early 1990s, more and more companies have been presenting their annual reports not merely in terms of financial performance—the traditional 'bottom line'—but also of their social and environmental achievements. For instance, they might have sponsored sportspeople for the Olympics and reduced their CO_2 emissions. This triple bottom lining—also known as the 3Ps approach, namely 'people, planet, and profit'—is usually presented as 'sustainability reporting'. But in recent years, there has been a push to add a fourth bottom line, governance. This would include reporting on what a company has been doing to reduce bribery and corruption. It is argued by proponents of this 'quadruple bottom lining' that firms would benefit from reporting a fourth line, since it should enhance a company's reputation. Although the evidence on this is mixed, some maintain that a company will lose market share if it develops a bad reputation: whether this is true or not, many firms factor in 'reputational risk' when making important decisions.

Civil society, domestic and international

While the concept of civil society can be traced back to Aristotle, it became a significant item on the social science agenda back in the

18th century. The term has since had a patchy history, and there is still disagreement on what it means. For our purposes, since the role of the business sector has already been considered, the other principal components of civil society analysed will be the mass media, non-government organizations (NGOs), and social media.

In a well-functioning democratic system, the mass media, both print and electronic, have a significant role to play in combating corruption. They can investigate allegations and publish their findings, and both directly and indirectly pressure the authorities to pursue the claims. Unfortunately, the mass media in many countries do not enjoy the autonomy they should. In describing the diverse roles and nature the media can play, Rodney Tiffen uses a canine metaphor that classifies them into five possible categories: the watchdog (the ideal role of the media); the muzzled watchdog (the media are severely constrained, not only by censorship, but also by defamation laws that are heavily skewed towards the interests of those the media are accusing of misconduct); the lapdog (the media allow themselves to be manipulated by political elites); the yapping pack (the media make a lot of noise, often copy each other, but are neither investigating cases properly nor playing a constructive role); and the wolf (the most dangerous type, in which the media are careless about investigating allegations properly, and publish irresponsibly, thereby increasing public cynicism and undermining system legitimacy).

It is clear from Tiffen's typology that the role the media play in combating corruption may be limited or even negative. An example of the latter, and of the 'muzzled watchdog' scenario, is the introduction in Russia in 2013 of a law that prohibits the media from publishing details of the private assets of members of the families of senior officials. There have been allegations that members of the Moscow political elite have improperly registered property in the names of members of their families—including children—so as to hide some of their own wealth; whether or not this is true, any media outlet that sought to investigate this and publish its findings would face potential litigation.

Although the first use of the term NGO has been traced back to 1945, the acronym has only been in popular use since the 1970s, and has become far more familiar since the 1990s. There are numerous types of NGO; we shall consider only those domestic and international ones committed to combating corruption.

The best-known international anti-corruption NGO is Berlin-based TI, which is global, but has local branches ('national chapters') in many countries. The mastermind behind this, Peter Eigen, had been managing World Bank operations in East Africa, and became increasingly incensed at the ways in which corrupt local elites were taking for themselves international funding that was meant to help the poor. This led him to establish TI in 1993; he chaired the organization from then until 2005.

In addition to the various indices of corruption considered in earlier chapters, TI also produces practical 'toolkits'. Aware that a 'one-size-fits-all' approach to combating corruption in diverse cultures and agencies is inappropriate, TI sensibly prefers to identify and explain various methods (tools) that it makes available to those people or organizations wanting to fight corruption to choose from, according to local needs and circumstances.

One other TI initiative is the promotion since the 1990s of 'Integrity Pacts' in public procurement. In TI's own words, integrity pacts are 'essentially an agreement between the government agency offering a contract and the companies bidding for it that they will abstain from bribery, collusion and other corrupt practices for the extent of the contract'; they incorporate a monitoring system whereby NGOs (often the local TI chapter) will seek to check on the extent to which the signatories to the integrity pact comply with it in practice.

Another international NGO is the U4 Anti-Corruption Resource Centre, established in 2002 and based in Bergen, Norway. This has a somewhat different focus from TI's, in that it is primarily oriented to assisting (mainly European) donor organizations reduce corruption relating to their development aid programmes. This said, it works closely with TI, which runs U4's Help Desk from its Berlin headquarters. Other NGOs and NGO alliances with an international spread include Global Witness and Global Integrity.

There are also many individual domestically-based anti-corruption NGOs in most countries of the world. Many of these—more than 350 organizations from more than 100 countries—are linked with each other through the UNCAC Coalition. This was established in 2006 to coordinate the work and share best practice experiences of the various NGOs. Another global network is Publish What You Pay, which has a membership of more than 800 civil society organizations worldwide, and which focuses on corruption and other malpractices in the extractive industry sector.

To this point, the focus has been on formally organized agencies that make anti-corruption either their principal or a major objective. But sometimes, even more powerful than these agencies is the general public. A simple way in which ordinary citizens can fight corruption is by reporting known or suspected cases, or simply making suggestions on how to combat it; while this often involves technology, such as access to a telephone or a computer, it need not (see Figure 6). Another is for members of the public to refuse to pay bribes. Unfortunately, this can sometimes be easier said than done: if the only way to secure potentially life-saving medical treatment for oneself or one's family is to offer bribes to doctors who are supposed to provide free healthcare, it is understandable that many will do so.

But there are other ways in which the public can play an important role. Social media are becoming increasingly significant

6. **A Kenyan anti-corruption suggestion box: combating corruption can include low-tech methods.**

in all sorts of areas, including anti-corruption. In Russia, the best-known blogger on corruption, particularly in public procurement, is Alexander Navalnyi. His critical blogs have resonated with so many Russians that he was at one time considered a strong possibility to run for president in 2018. At the global level, Facebook now has a 'Name and shame your corrupt politicians and Public Servants' facility.

7. Mass protests against corruption are increasingly common in many parts of the world.

In his 2012 book on corruption, Frank Vogl emphasized the role of 'tweeting', which he saw as a major factor in raising political awareness in some of the countries that experienced the so-called Arab Spring, and as a potentially powerful weapon in fighting corruption. There is no question that tweeting can rapidly mobilize thousands of people to protest against various forms of injustice, including corruption; it has played a role in recent years in galvanizing citizens to participate in mass protests against corruption in Argentina, Brazil, Bulgaria, India, Thailand, Turkey, Ukraine, the US, and many other countries (Figure 7). While some mass demonstrations have led to regime collapse, others have resulted in harsh clampdowns. But in the latter case, regimes typically reduce their own legitimacy, making their eventual demise even more likely.

Criticisms of anti-corruption

It is clear from this chapter that international interest in corruption is only some two decades old. In that time, the anti-corruption movement has grown almost exponentially. However, this development has attracted criticism from some quarters, for two main reasons.

First, some accuse the international anti-corruption movement—or at least part of it—of 'cultural imperialism'. There is no question that some aspects of the movement are highly intrusive, and interfere with a country's sovereignty. But it should be acknowledged that this is often done because of the perceived high levels of corruption in that country, about which many of its citizens are angry, but feel helpless to do anything. Surveys reveal that the general public is often grateful to outside agencies for pressuring its elites to become less corrupt, especially if this means that foreign aid will flow to those who most need it.

Second, a growing number of critics, most of them academics, claim that the fight against corruption has resulted in the emergence of an anti-corruption 'industry' that has a vested interest in creating as many new jobs in anti-corruption as possible and making the corruption situation appear as dire as it can. If anti-corruption NGOs and state-sponsored ACAs are highly successful in reducing corruption, the critics maintain, they may appear to have made themselves redundant, and will lose funding or even be disbanded. In a sense, then, the anti-corruption industry is being accused of itself being corrupt.

There is unquestionably some truth to this argument. Yet it cannot go unchallenged. For instance, only if it is assumed that corruption has been finally eradicated, or, more realistically, *permanently* reduced to 'manageable' levels, does the argument about the superfluity of anti-corruption bodies hold. In the real world, corruption is constantly reappearing in various guises, and disbanding agencies designed to combat it is likely to result in its renewed growth.

There is thus a real danger of throwing the baby out with the bathwater when criticizing the anti-corruption industry. While it is vital to ensure that anti-corruption bodies are efficient, answerable, and transparent, the many negative—sometimes fatal—effects of corruption must never be forgotten. Too many commentators are strident critics, yet make few if any positive proposals for combating a very real problem.

So what works?

Having considered in this and the previous chapter many of the methods available for combating corruption, we can now address what is in many ways the most important question—which methods are the most effective? Unfortunately, every method outlined has its drawbacks; space limitations require selectivity in analysing these, and we shall here concentrate on the effectiveness of international efforts, since several domestic approaches were assessed in the previous chapter. Have the numerous conventions, etc. had any noticeable effect, or are they in practice little more than rhetoric?

Despite the various EU and CoE targeted programmes, corruption remains a serious problem in most post-communist countries. Moreover, the first ever *European Union Integrity System* report, published in 2014, made it clear that EU institutions remain susceptible to corruption because of loopholes in regulations and poor implementation of ethics policies.

According to a 2013 official report on the implementation of the OECD anti-bribery convention, '30 of the 40 countries signed up to the convention are barely investigating and prosecuting foreign bribery, considering the large value of their exports', which is a depressing finding. While Japan has ratified the convention, it has been criticized on various occasions for doing too little in practice. And while the UK has now been praised for its particularly tough

Corruption

stand against corporate bribery in its 2010 legislation, it had previously been criticized for doing very little in terms of implementing the OECD Convention.

Moreover, there is a real danger of backsliding here. In the first decade after the introduction of the OECD Convention, the US and Germany proved to be particularly good citizens (and by 2013 had been joined by the UK and Switzerland), in the sense of using their Convention-based laws to prosecute a relatively large number of companies. But, as TI often points out in its annual assessments of the implementation of the OECD Convention, if 'good guys' like the US and Germany see other countries getting away with doing very little to abide by their Convention commitments, they will surely ask themselves sooner or later if it is fair for them to punish their own companies, and thereby hand business to firms from states that are essentially paying lip service to the Convention. If the answer is negative, they may stop being model citizens.

In the case of UNCAC, the monitoring process is very recent, beginning with a five-year 'first review cycle' in 2010; since this is not due for completion until 2015, it is too early to determine its success. But when it is recalled that UNCAC has been in effect since 2005, one must question why it takes so long to evaluate its effectiveness. Moreover, some of the world's leading trading nations—notably Germany and Japan—have not even ratified UNCAC yet. And just how powerful is UNCAC anyway? In theory, states that *have* ratified it can be taken to court (the UN's International Court of Justice) for non-compliance; in practice, the ICJ has essentially no enforcement power.

Turning to the World Bank's considerable efforts—it has already been shown how its tracking surveys can substantially reduce corruption. But a major criticism it has faced in the past is that its tough policy on cancelling projects in which it has detected significant corruption hurts those most in need of its assistance. Another issue is that its debarment list mostly targets individuals and small companies; it seems that powerful TNCs often get away with misconduct in a way that relatively powerless firms and individuals cannot. And a 2011 internal review of the bank's anti-corruption efforts reported mixed results. While there had been some success in strengthening ACAs in many countries, the report found that the bank was falling far short of its own anti-corruption objectives.

Do all these disappointing facts mean that the fight against corruption since the 1990s has in essence been a waste of time and effort? There are certainly some 'big names' in corruption studies who come close to arguing this. Thus the man who was at one time in charge of corruption and governance analysis at the World Bank, Daniel Kaufmann, concluded in 2005 that a decade of global anti-corruption efforts had little to show, and in 2009 described the effort being made to combat corruption as 'tepid'. In introducing the 2013 CPI, TI Chair Huguette Labelle pointed out that 'The Corruption Perceptions Index 2013 demonstrates that all countries still face the threat of corruption at all levels of government, from the issuing of local permits to the enforcement of laws and regulations'; according to that CPI, almost 70 per cent of countries scored below 50 (in the 0–100 scale), suggesting high levels of corruption in them.

Despite these depressing results and the criticisms, there are *some* encouraging signs. In a 2014 book, Michael Johnston pointed out:

> That they—we—are still searching for ways to control corruption in diverse societies does not mean the movement has failed: after all, a generation ago corruption was not even widely discussed...Today's heightened awareness, in itself, is a major accomplishment.

Moreover, while there is unquestionably some truth in U4's (website) claim that 'Evidence on what works and why is sparse in anti-corruption', comparative analysis has revealed *some* guidelines that should be adhered to everywhere if anti-corruption is to progress. One of the most obvious lessons is that the question of whether 'many hands make light work' or 'too many cooks spoil the broth' can now be answered; as Jon Quah has pointed out, the Singaporean and Hong Kong successes in fighting corruption are to no small extent related to the fact that they both have single, powerful, and independent ACAs. Where there are multiple agencies, there are usually overlapping and often conflicting responsibilities, which result in problems of coordination and buck-passing; there are typically also huge inefficiencies and wasted resources.

Many analysts maintain that the ultimate success or otherwise of anti-corruption measures depends on political will. This point is persuasive as far as it goes, but needs to be unpacked and expanded. For instance, *whose* will are we talking about? Many cultures and languages have the phrase 'a fish rots from the head', meaning that corruption will be worse where the political elite sets a bad example. In this sense, it might seem that the will of the leadership is all-important. But while this is crucial, it is not the only will that matters. A leadership may be genuinely committed to fighting corruption, but nevertheless have insufficient control over its own bureaucracy to turn this commitment into reality. Moreover, in a neo-liberal globalized world, there is a limit to the power of political leaders to control TNCs.

So we can now refine the point about political will. Political leaderships must not only be genuinely committed, i.e. have the political will to combat corruption, but must also have the *capacity* to implement their will. In addition, the numerous parties involved—state officials, the corporate sector, IOs, civil society, and individual members of the public—also need to have the will to combat corruption. The relative weight of the role to be played by each of these actors varies, and will do so from country to country. Nevertheless, each has an important role.

In Chapter 6, it was pointed out that corruption is a wicked problem. It will never completely disappear: as Tacitus noted centuries ago, almost as soon as legislators produce new laws to combat fraud and corruption, the dishonest devise ways to circumvent them. But corruption appears to be much less of a problem in some countries than in others: for example, small affluent states with a robust democracy, a strong commitment to the rule of law, high levels of trust, and a well-developed civil society apparently have less corruption, which demonstrates that it can be reduced to manageable levels.

Nevertheless, the short-term outlook is not bright. The rule of law and a vibrant civil society are both associated with well-functioning democracies. While the World Justice Project's *WJP Rule of Law Index* for 2014 suggested that the corruption situation had improved slightly over the previous year, what is now arguably the most authoritative guide to the overall level of democracy around the world, the Economist Intelligence Unit's *Democracy Index* (almost annual since 2007) had the subtitles 'Democracy under Stress' and 'Democracy at a Standstill' for the 2011 and 2012 editions respectively. Moreover, that the essentially amoral neo-liberal ideology, with its emphasis on ends over means and blurring of the distinctions between the state and the market, still dominates the global economy—despite the hopes of scholars such as Colin Crouch that the Global Financial Crisis would change this—bodes ill. There is still a long way to go in the fight against corruption.

Further reading

General

Almost all IO and NGO documentation cited in this book is freely available on the internet, and only sources that might be difficult to locate without full publication details are included here, along with sources not referred to in the text that should be particularly useful to newcomers. An excellent general introduction to corruption is C. Fletcher and D. Herrmann, *The Internationalisation of Corruption* (Gower, 2012), while an older standard work is A. Heidenheimer and M. Johnston (eds.), *Political Corruption*, 3rd edn. (Transaction, 2001). Readers particularly interested in economic aspects of corruption should see the two-volume collection edited by Susan Rose-Ackerman (the 2nd volume co-edited with Tina Søreide), the *International Handbook on the Economics of Corruption* (Elgar, vol. 1, 2006, vol. 2, 2011). An older but still invaluable collection that covers both theoretical approaches and the situation in many countries of the world is the four-volume collection edited by R. Williams and various co-editors, *Corruption in the Developing World* (with R. Theobold), *Corruption in the Developed World* (with J. Moran and R. Flanary), *Controlling Corruption* (with A. Doig) and, without a co-editor, *Explaining Corruption* (all four volumes published by Elgar, 2000). For broad analyses covering regions and continents see C. Blake and S. Morris (eds.), *Corruption and Democracy in Latin America* (University of Pittsburgh Press, 2009); D. Della Porta and Y. Mény (eds.), *Democracy and Corruption in Europe* (Pinter, 1997); J. Hatchard, *Combating Corruption* (Elgar, 2014; on Africa); L. Holmes, *Rotten States?* (Duke University Press, 2006; on post-Communist transition states); T. Lindsey and H. Dick (eds.), *Corruption in Asia* (Federation Press, 2002); Ting Gong and S. Ma (eds.), *Preventing Corruption in Asia* (Routledge, 2009); C. Warner, *The Best System Money Can Buy* (Cornell University Press, 2007; on the European Union): there is room for a comparative collection on the Middle East, but a starting point is H. Askari, S. Rehman, and N. Arfaa, *Corruption and its Manifestation in the Persian Gulf* (Elgar, 2010). For a recent collection that, *inter alia*, focuses on corruption in different sectors and branches, see A. Graycar and R. Smith (eds.), *Handbook of Global Research and Practice in Corruption* (Elgar, 2011). The single most useful journal on corruption is *Crime, Law and Social Change*, while an invaluable website is Transparency International's.

Chapter 1: What is corruption?

Two of the best introductions to the problems of defining corruption are M. Philp in *Political Studies*, 45 (3), 1997: 436–62 and K. Sass Mikkelsen in *Crime, Law and Social Change*, 60 (4), 2013: 357–74. On corruption's role in the collapse of the Roman Empire see R. MacMullen, *Corruption and the Decline of Rome* (Yale University Press, 1990), while for Roman, Ancient Greek, and other interpretations of corruption to the late 18th century see B. Buchan and L. Hill, *An Intellectual History of Political Corruption* (Palgrave Macmillan, 2014). The best analysis of *blat* is A. Ledeneva's *Russia's Economy of Favours* (Cambridge University Press, 1998); on *guanxi*, see T. Gold, D. Guthrie, and D. Wank (eds.), *Social Connections in China* (Cambridge University Press, 2002). Arnold Heidenheimer's threefold distinctions are in A. Heidenheimer (ed.), *Political Corruption* (Holt, Rinehart and Winston, 1970): 3–28. The World Bank definitions of 'state capture' and 'administrative corruption' are from J. Hellman, G. Jones, and D. Kaufmann, *World Bank Policy Research Working Papers*, no. 2444, 2000, while Rasma Karklins' typology is in her book *The State Made Me Do It* (M. E. Sharpe, 2005). For a standard analysis of the history of bribery see J. Noonan, *Bribes* (University of California Press, 1987).

Chapter 2: Why corruption is a problem

Many of the effects of corruption outlined in this chapter are analysed in detail in S. Rose-Ackerman, *Corruption and Government* (Cambridge University Press, 1999). The 1998 IMF Working Paper on corruption and inequality cited is S. Gupta, H. Davoodi, and R. Alonso-Terme, 'Does Corruption Affect Income Inequality and Poverty?'; an updated version is in *Economics of Governance*, 3 (1), 2001: 23–45. A more detailed analysis of the links between corruption and inequality (and trust) is Eric Uslaner's *Corruption, Inequality and the Rule of Law* (Cambridge University Press, 2008). The article by Osita Agbu is in *West Africa Review*, 4 (1), 2003: 1–13; further analyses of corruption's role in human trafficking are by S. Zhang and S. Pineda, in D. Siegel and H. Nelen (eds.), *Organized Crime: Culture, Markets and Policies* (Springer, 2008): 41–55; and K. Skrivankova, G. Dell, E. Larson, M. Adomeit, and S. Albert, *The Role of Corruption in Trafficking in Persons* (UNODC, 2011). A useful introduction to corruption in the 'legitimate' arms trade is A. Feinstein, *Shadow World* (Penguin, 2012). Those interested in corporate misconduct in the US could start with M. Clinard and P. Yeager, *Corporate Crime* (Free Press, 1980; rev. edn. 2005) or the more recent A. Huffington, *Pigs at the Trough* (Three Rivers, 2009); for broader coverage see H. Pontell and G. Geis (eds.), *International Handbook of White-Collar and Corporate Crime* (Springer, 2010). The relationship between corruption and economic crises is analysed by L. Holmes, in R. Pettman (ed.), *A Handbook of International Political Economy* (World Scientific Publishing, 2012): 211–28. On the connection between buildings collapsing and corruption, see N. Ambraseys and R. Bilham in *Nature*, 469 (7329), 2011: 153–5. On corruption and the environment, two useful sources are *Corruption, Environment and the United Nations Convention against Corruption* (UNODC, 2012) and L. Pellegrini, *Corruption, Development and the Environment* (Springer, 2011). Paolo Mauro's article is in *Quarterly Journal of Economics*, 110 (3), 1995: 681–712, while S.-J. Wei's is in *The Review of Economics and Statistics*, 82 (1), 2000: 1–11. Wei's approach has been challenged by Barry Hindess, in L. de Sousa, P. Larmour, and B. Hindess (eds.), *Governments, NGOs and Anti-Corruption* (Routledge, 2009): 19–32. Readers interested in corruption and party financing (mainly in established democracies) should see I. McMenamin, *If Money Talks, What Does it Say?* (Oxford University Press, 2013). The Frank Vogl reference is from his *Waging War on Corruption* (Rowman and Littlefield, 2012). On corruption (broadly understood) in soccer see D. Hill, *The Insider's Guide to Match-Fixing in Football* (Anne McDermid, 2013). For the 1960s revisionist sources cited in the text see the entries by Leff, Nye, Huntington, and Leys in Heidenheimer and Johnston 2001 (cited previously). Ivan Krastev's argument is in *East European Constitutional Review*, 7 (3), 1998: 56–8, while that of Manzetti and Wilson is in *Comparative Political Studies*, 40 (8), 2007: 949–70. Klitgaard's approach is in his book *Controlling Corruption*, 2nd edn. (University of California Press, 1991; 1st edn. 1988).

Chapter 3: Can we measure corruption?

Two comprehensive analyses of the methods used for measuring corruption are C. Sampford, A. Shacklock, C. Connors, and F. Galtung (eds.), *Measuring Corruption* (Ashgate, 2006) and R. June, A. Chowdhury, N. Heller, and J. Werve, *A User's Guide to Measuring Corruption* (UNDP, 2008). Moisés Naím's article is in *Brown Journal of World Affairs*, 2 (2), 1995: 245–61. On PETS in Uganda and Tanzania see G. Sundet in *U4 Issue*, 8, 2008, while the methodology of tracking surveys is explained in R. Reinikka and J. Svensson, *World Bank Policy Research Working Paper*, 3071, 2003. On the latest developments in and advocacy of the proxy method see J. Johnsøn and P. Mason, *U4 Brief*, 2, 2013. A valuable study of experimentation for measuring and classifying corruption is D. Serra and L. Wantchekon, *New Advances in Experimental Research on Corruption* (Emerald, 2012), while a highly innovative experiment relating explicitly to money-laundering is M. Findley, D. Nielson, and J. Sharman, *Global Shell Games* (Cambridge University Press, 2014).

Chapter 4: Psycho-social and cultural explanations

The classic analysis of structuration theory is A. Giddens, *The Constitution of Society* (Polity, 1984). The 'sucker mentality' is discussed in J. Finckenauer and E. Waring, *Russian Mafia in America* (Northeastern University Press, 1998), while the original version of opportunity theory is in R. Cloward and L. Ohlin, *Delinquency and Opportunity*, 2nd edn. (Free Press, 1963). Still the best analysis of rational choice theory is D. Green and I. Shapiro's *Pathologies of Rational Choice Theory* (Yale University Press, 1994). For the original version of labelling theory see H. Becker, *Outsiders*, updated edn. (Free Press, 1973), while the closely related shaming theory is in J. Braithwaite, *Crime, Shame and Reintegration* (Cambridge University Press, 1989). The original version of control theory outlined here is from T. Hirschi, *Causes of Delinquency* (University of California Press, 1969); the later general theory of crime is in

M. Gottfredson and T. Hirschi, *A General Theory of Crime* (Stanford University Press, 1990). There is a brief overview of historical and other cultural explanations of corruption in R. Goel and M. Nelson, *BOFIT Discussion Papers*, no. 6 (Bank of Finland Institute of Economies in Transition, 2008). For statistically-based analyses of the weak relationship between religion and corruption see D. Treisman in *Journal of Public Economics*, 76 (3), 2000: 399–457 and R. LaPorta, F. Lopez-de-Silanes, A. Shleifer, and R. Vishny in *Journal of Law, Economics and Organization*, 15 (1), 1999: 222–79. The work cited from Gardner is in *Economic History of Developing Regions*, 25 (2), 2010: 213–36, while another analysis of the relationship between the colonial legacy and corruption can be found in the Treisman article cited previously. On the effect of legal cultures on corruption see S. Rose-Ackerman, in D. Rodriguez and L. Ehrichs (eds.), *Global Corruption Report 2007* (Cambridge University Press, 2007): 15–24. The Ledeneva quotation cited is from her 1998 book cited previously. The article by Fisman and Miguel is in *Journal of Political Economy*, 115 (6), 2007: 1020–48. Sajó's argument is in *East European Constitutional Review*, 7 (2), 1998: 37–46, while a good example of the 'underworld'/'upperworld' distinction is Vincenzo Ruggiero's *Organized and Corporate Crime in Europe* (Dartmouth, 1996). Works on corruption by Syed Hussein Alatas include *Corruption* (Avebury, 1990) and *Corruption and the Destiny of Asia* (Prentice-Hall, 1999). A standard critique of the cultural approach to explaining miscreant behaviour is J. Ferrell, K. Hayward, and J. Young, *Cultural Criminology* (Sage, 1998).

Chapter 5: System-related explanations

The arguments and data-sources cited in this chapter concerning the relationship between government involvement in the economy and corruption are V. Tanzi, in *Finance & Development*, 32 (4), 1995: 24–6; J. Gerring and S. Thacker, in *International Organization*, 59 (1), 2005: 233–54; K. Schwab, *The Global Competitiveness Report 2012–2013* (World Economic Forum, 2012); D. Hall, in *Development in Practice*, 9 (5), 1999: 539–56; K. Ohmae, *The Borderless World*, rev. edn. (HarperBusiness, 1999); R. Klitgaard, *Controlling Corruption* (cited previously), and, for the formulaic version, *Finance and Development*, 35 (1), 1998: 3–6. The case of the Indian tax collectors is referred to in D. Mookherjee and I. Png, *Economic Journal*, 105 (428), 1995: 145–59. For dismissal of the notion that larger government necessarily means more corruption see R. LaPorta, F. Lopez-de-Silanes, A. Shleifer, and R. Vishny, *Journal of Law, Economics and Organization*, 15 (1), 1999: 222–79, while the connections between corruption and outsourcing are considered in J. O'Looney, *Outsourcing State and Local Government Services* (Quorum, 1998). On the relationship between globalization and corruption, with particular reference to money-laundering, see L. Cockcroft, *Global Corruption: Money, Power and Ethics in the Modern World* (Tauris, 2012). On the relationship between GDP per capita and corruption see You Jong-sung and Sanjeev Khagram in *American Sociological Review*, 70 (1), 2005: 136–57. The connections between corruption and international trade are considered in P. Dutt, *Canadian Journal of Economics*, 42 (1), 2009: 155–83. The reference cited concerning government size is G. Kotera, K. Okada, and Sovannroeun Samreth, *Economic Modelling*, 29 (6), 2012: 2340–8. Hellman and Kaufmann's point is in *Finance and Development*, 38 (3), 2001: 1–8; alternative views on the relationship between business and government can be found in S. Rose-Ackerman's 1999 book (cited previously), and D. Bowser, in D. Lovell (ed.), *The Transition* (Ashgate, 2002): 80–95. A counter-intuitive but interesting analysis relating current corruption levels to educational levels in 1870 is E. Uslaner and B. Rothstein, *Quality of Government Working Paper*, no. 2012/5 (Gothenburg, 2012). The articles cited on the relationship between gender and corruption are D. Dollar, R. Fisman, and R. Gatti, in *Journal of Economic Behavior & Organization*, 46 (4), 2001: 423–9; and H.-E. Sung, in *Crime, Law and Social Change*, 58 (3), 2012: 195–219. The Treisman quotation is from *Annual Review of Political Science*, 10, 2007: 211–44.

Chapter 6: What can states do?

For a substantial, if slightly dated, collection on combating corruption see R. Williams and A. Doig (eds.), *Controlling Corruption* (Elgar, 2000), while the even older single authored *Controlling Corruption* by R. Klitgaard (cited previously) remains a standard work.

On Singapore and Hong Kong (as well as other states with low levels of corruption) see J. Quah (ed.), *Different Paths to Curbing Corruption* (Emerald, 2013). On the Filipino case see W. Cragg and W. Woof, in W. Cragg (ed.), *Ethics Codes, Corporations and the Challenge of*

Globalization (Elgar, 2005): 1–43, while those interested in how miscreant corporations could be better controlled might start with S. Simpson, *Corporate Crime, Law, and Social Control* (Cambridge University Press, 2002). The notion that higher salaries lead to less corruption is challenged in the article by LaPorta et al. cited previously. The German rotation experiment is analysed in K. Abbink, *European Journal of Political Economy*, 20 (4), 2004: 887–906, while the research conducted in India is described by F. de Zwart, in H. Bakker and N. Schulte Nordholt (eds.), *Corruption and Legitimacy* (SISWO, 1996): 53–64. Olken's experiment in Indonesia is summarized in *Journal of Political Economy*, 117 (2), 2007: 200–49. On anti-corruption campaigns, mainly in developing and transition states, see S. Bracking (ed.), *Corruption and Development* (Palgrave Macmillan, 2007), although the contributors often adopt a broader approach to 'campaigns' than that adopted here.

For the argument that equally balancing male and female officers is the optimal arrangement see R. Mukherjee and O. Gokcekus, in R. Hodess, T. Inowlocki, D. Rodriguez, and T. Wolfe (eds.), *Global Corruption Report 2004* (Pluto, 2004): 337–9, while the claim that more women in politics reduces corruption is in D. Dollar et al. (2001), cited previously and A. Mason and E. King, *Engendering Development through Gender Equality in Rights, Resources, and Voice* (World Bank, 2001). Sung's challenge to this argument is in his 2012 article already cited. For Corsianos' argument, see *The Complexities of Police Corruption* (Rowman and Littlefield, 2012). On the Georgian anti-corruption efforts see A. Alam and V. R. Southworth (with others), *Fighting Corruption in Public Services: Chronicling Georgia's Reforms* (World Bank, 2012). The Peruvian police experiment and experience is analysed in S. Karim, *Americas Quarterly*, 5 (3), 2011: 42–6, while Bogotá's 'mime' experiment is described in R. Fisman and E. Miguel, *Economic Gangsters* (Princeton University Press, 2010).

Chapter 7: What else can be done?

On the role of various international agents covered in this chapter see S. Rose-Ackerman and P. Carrington (eds.), *Anti-Corruption Policy* (Carolina Academic Press, 2013). Useful overviews of many of the themes covered in Chapters 6 and 7 are F. Vogl's 2012 book (cited previously), and N. Kochan and R. Goodyear, *Corruption* (Palgrave Macmillan, 2011). The critical article by Peter Eigen is in *TI Q*

(September 2003: 1), while the more upbeat items mentioned are
P. Ala'I, in *Loyola University Chicago International Law Review*, 6 (1),
2008–9: 259–78 and P. M. Nichols in *New York University Journal of
International Law and Politics*, 28 (4), 1996: 711–84. On the World
Bank's anti-corruption efforts by 2008 see Independent Evaluation
Group, *Public Sector Reform: What Works and Why?* (World Bank,
2008): 58–65. A valuable study of how the role of donor countries and
IOs in supporting domestic ACAs in developing countries could be
improved is by A. Doig, D. Watt, and R. Williams in *U4 Report*, May
2005 (online). Tiffen's analysis of the roles of the media is in *Scandals,
Media and Corruption in Contemporary Australia* (University of New
South Wales Press, 1999), while Vogl's book is detailed above. Critical
analyses of the anti-corruption 'industry' can be found in D. Kennedy,
in *Connecticut Journal of International Law*, 14 (2), 1999: 455–65;
B. Michael and D. Bowser, *The Evolution of the Anti-Corruption
Industry in the Third Wave of Anti-Corruption Work* (bepress, 2009);
L. de Sousa, P. Larmour, and B. Hindess (2009, cited previously); and
S. Sampson, in *Global Crime*, 11 (2), 2010: 261–78. An interesting
variant on this is F. Anechiarico and J. Jacobs, *The Pursuit of Absolute
Integrity* (University of Chicago Press, 1996). For up-to-date analysis
and assessment of the OECD Convention see M. Pieth, L. Low, and
N. Bonucci (eds.), *The OECD Convention on Bribery*, 2nd edn.
(Cambridge University Press, 2014). Kaufmann's 2005 assessment is
in *Finance and Development*, 42 (3), September 2005 (online), while
his 'tepid' remark is in *Development Outreach*, February 2009: 26–9.
On the need to tailor approaches to specific contexts see J. E. Campos
and S. Pradhan (eds.), *The Many Faces of Corruption* (World Bank,
2007); M. Johnston, *Syndromes of Corruption* (Cambridge University
Press, 2005) and *Corruption, Contention and Reform* (Cambridge
University Press, 2014); the quote in this chapter is from the latter.
The argument that neo-liberalism was *not* seriously challenged by the
Global Financial Crisis is in Colin Crouch's *The Strange Non-Death of
Neoliberalism* (Polity, 2011).

Index

Index

INTERNATIONAL RELATIONS
A Very Short Introduction
Paul Wilkinson

Of undoubtable relevance today, in a post-9-11 world of growing political tension and unease, this *Very Short Introduction* covers the topics essential to an understanding of modern international relations. Paul Wilkinson explains the theories and the practice that underlies the subject, and investigates issues ranging from foreign policy, arms control, and terrorism, to the environment and world poverty. He examines the role of organizations such as the United Nations and the European Union, as well as the influence of ethnic and religious movements and terrorist groups which also play a role in shaping the way states and governments interact. This up-to-date book is required reading for those seeking a new perspective to help untangle and decipher international events.

www.oup.com/vsi

AMERICAN POLITICAL PARTIES AND ELECTIONS
A Very Short Introduction
Sandy L. Maisel

Few Americans and even fewer citizens of other nations understand the electoral process in the United States. Still fewer understand the role played by political parties in the electoral process or the ironies within the system. Participation in elections in the United States is much lower than in the vast majority of mature democracies. Perhaps this is because of the lack of competition in a country where only two parties have a true chance of winning, despite the fact that a large number of citizens claim allegiance to neither and think badly of both. Studying these factors, you begin to get a very clear picture indeed of the problems that underlay this much trumpeted electoral system.

CHRISTIAN ETHICS
A Very Short Introduction
D. Stephen Long

This *Very Short Introduction* to Christian ethics introduces the topic by examining its sources and historical basis. D. Stephen Long presents a discussion of the relationship between Christian ethics, modern, and postmodern ethics, and explores practical issues including sex, money, and power. Long recognises the inherent difficulties in bringing together 'Christian' and 'ethics' but argues that this is an important task for both the Christian faith and for ethics. Arguing that Christian ethics are not a precise science, but the cultivation of practical wisdom from a range of sources, Long also discusses some of the failures of the Christian tradition, including the crusades, the conquest, slavery, inquisitions, and the Galileo affair.

www.oup.com/vsi

GLOBALIZATION
A Very Short Introduction
Manfred Steger

'Globalization' has become one of the defining buzzwords of our time - a term that describes a variety of accelerating economic, political, cultural, ideological, and environmental processes that are rapidly altering our experience of the world. It is by its nature a dynamic topic - and this *Very Short Introduction* has been fully updated for 2009, to include developments in global politics, the impact of terrorism, and environmental issues. Presenting globalization in accessible language as a multifaceted process encompassing global, regional, and local aspects of social life, Manfred B. Steger looks at its causes and effects, examines whether it is a new phenomenon, and explores the question of whether, ultimately, globalization is a good or a bad thing.

HUMAN RIGHTS
A Very Short Introduction
Andrew Clapham

An appeal to human rights in the face of injustice can be a heartfelt and morally justified demand for some, while for others it remains merely an empty slogan. Taking an international perspective and focusing on highly topical issues such as torture, arbitrary detention, privacy, health and discrimination, this *Very Short Introduction* will help readers to understand for themselves the controversies and complexities behind this vitally relevant issue. Looking at the philosophical justification for rights, the historical origins of human rights and how they are formed in law, Andrew Clapham explains what our human rights actually are, what they might be, and where the human rights movement is heading.

www.oup.com/vsi

INTERNATIONAL MIGRATION
A Very Short Introduction
Khalid Koser

Why has international migration become an issue of such intense public and political concern? How closely linked are migrants with terrorist organizations? What factors lie behind the dramatic increase in the number of women migrating? This *Very Short Introduction* examines the phenomenon of international human migration - both legal and illegal. Taking a global look at politics, economics, and globalization, the author presents the human side of topics such as asylum and refugees, human trafficking, migrant smuggling, development, and the international labour force.

www.oup.com/vsi

ORGANIZATIONS
A Very Short Introduction
Mary Jo Hatch

This *Very Short Introductions* addresses all of these questions and considers many more. Mary Jo Hatch introduces the concept of organizations by presenting definitions and ideas drawn from the a variety of subject areas including the physical sciences, economics, sociology, psychology, anthropology, literature, and the visual and performing arts. Drawing on examples from prehistory and everyday life, from the animal kingdom as well as from business, government, and other formal organizations, Hatch provides a lively and thought provoking introduction to the process of organization.

www.oup.com/vsi